"Throughout history, there have been countless gifted individuals called 'sensitives' or 'psychics' who have provided definitions, theories and descriptions of human aura. Science has repeatedly rejected this vast storehouse of psychic testimony since the methods of producing this information have been unorthodox and generally seen as impossible. People, for example, who claimed to have seen a luminous energy sphere around a human body have been highly suspect, especially if they also claimed the ability to diagnose illness by interpreting the colors and patterns of this mysterious emanation.

When news of a Soviet technique perfected by Semyon Kirlian, capable of photographing energy patterns around plant leaves, small objects such as coins and even human fingertips reached the West, many people felt that at last they would have proof that the aura was real."

the
Human Aura

Edited by
Nicholas M. Regush

A BERKLEY MEDALLION BOOK
published by
BERKLEY PUBLISHING CORPORATION

FOR JAN MERTA

Berkley Publishing Corporation
200 Madison Avenue
New York, New York 10016

SBN 425-02733-3

BERKLEY MEDALLION BOOKS are published by
Berkley Publishing Corporation
200 Madison Avenue
New York, N.Y. 10016

BERKLEY MEDALLION BOOKS ® TM 757,375

Printed in the United States of America

Berkley Medallion Edition, DECEMBER, 1974

CONTENTS

the
Human Aura

LIST OF SOURCES FOR SELECTIONS

1. "Paracelsus on the 'Vital Force' and Medicine" by Frantz Hartmann. From: *The Life and The Doctrines of Paracelsus*, John W. Lowell Co., New York, 1891.

2. "Principles" by Franz Anton Mesmer. From: *Animal Magnetism and The Life Energy* copyright © 1974 by Jerome Eden. Reprinted by permission of Exposition Press, Hicksville, New York.

3. "Od" by Baron Karl Von Reichenbach. From: *Letters on Od and Magnetism*, Hutchinson & Co., London, 1926.

4. "The Aura Made Visible by the Aid of Chemical Screens" by Walter J. Kilner. From: *The Aura*, Samuel Weiser, Inc., New York, 1973.

5. "The Appearance of the Normal Aura" by Oscar Bagnall. From: *The Origins and Properties of the Human Aura*, copyright © 1970. Reprinted by permission of University Books, New York.

6. "The Energy Field" by John C. Pierrakos. From: *The Energy Field in Man and Nature*, Institute of Bioenergetic Analysis, New York.

7. "Developing Auric Sight" by S. G. J. Ouseley. From: *The Science of the Aura*, copyright © 1949. Reprinted by permission of L. N. Fowler & Co. Ltd., London.

8. "Auras" by Edgar Cayce. From: *Auras*, copyright © 1945. Reprinted by permission of A. R. E. Press, Virginia Beach.

9. "Types of Aura" by Ursula Roberts. From: *The Mystery of the Human Aura*. Reprinted by permission of

The Spiritualist Association of Great Britain, London, 1972.

10. "The Etheric Double" by Arthur E. Powell. From: *The Etheric Double*, copyright © 1969. Reprinted by permission of The Theosophical Publishing House, London.

11. "The Health Aura" by Charles Webster Leadbeater. From: *Man Visible and Invisible*, copyright © 1925. Reprinted by permission of The Theosophical Publishing House, Adyar, Madras, India.

12. "The Astral Body" by Sylvan Muldoon and Hereward Carrington. From: *The Phenomena of Astral Projection*, copyright © 1969. Reprinted by permission of Samuel Weiser, Inc., New York.

13. "Not With a Wand, Nor Lightly" by Robert A. Monroe. From: *Journeys Out of the Body*, copyright © 1971 by Robert A. Monroe. Reprinted by permission of Doubleday & Co., New York.

14. "Thought-Forms" by Annie Besant and Charles Webster Leadbeater. From *Thought-Forms*, copyright © 1925. Reprinted by permission of The Theosophical Publishing House, Adyar, Madras, India.

15. "Aura and the Séance" by Phoebe D. Payne and Laurence J. Bendit. From: *This World and That*, copyright © 1950. Faber and Faber, London. Reprinted by permission of Laurencee J. Bendit.

16. "The Brittle Aura" by Rosicrucian Wisdom Teachings. From: *The Mystery of the Human Aura*. Reprinted by permission of Society of Rosicrucians, Inc., New York.

17. "The Scientific Study of the Human Aura" by

Charles T. Tart. From: *Journal of the Society for Psychical Research*, 46:751, 1972. Reprinted by permission of Charles T. Hart.

18. "Energy Fields and Medical Diagnosis" by Shafica Karagulla. From Breakthrough to Creativity. Reprinted by permission of DeVorss & Co., Santa Monica, 1967.

19. "Are Psychoenergetic Pictures Possible?" by William A. Tiller. From: *New Scientist*, 62:895, London, 1974.

20. "The Schlieran System—An Aura Detector?" by Sheila Ostrander and Lynn Schroeder. From: *Handbook of Psi Discoveries*, copyright © 1974 by Sheila Ostrander and Lynn Shroeder. Reprinted by permission of Berkley Publishing Corporation, New York.

21. "Wilhelm Reich and Orgone: The Background" by W. E. Mann. From: *Orgone, Reich and Eros*, copyright © 1973 by W. Edward Mann. Reprinted by permission of Simon and Schuster, New York.

22. "Electro-Dynamic Man" by Vincent H. Gaddis. From: *Mysterious Fires and Lights*, copyright © 1967. by Vincent H. Gaddis. Reprinted by permission of David McKay Co. Inc., New York.

23. "My Faith" by Gustaf Strömberg. From: *The Soul of the Universe*. Reprinted by permission of Educational Research Institute, No. Hollywood, Calif., 1948.

24. "Ghost Universe" by James Sutherland. From: *Vertex*, 2:2, 1974. Reprinted by permission of James Sutherland.

INTRODUCTION

SCIENTISTS AND PSYCHICS

I

We live in the midst of awesome materialism. Our consumer society, aggressively promoted by the corporate world via the mass media, dictates a vast array of wants and hopes. Our practical everyday life has been so deeply rooted in this reality that conceiving of and exploring alternative ways of thinking has been extremely difficult. It has generally required an extraordinary act of will and critical self-examination.

The recent explosion of public interest in paranormal (or psi) phenomena such as telepathy and clairvoyance must be interpreted in the above context. It comes at a time when more people are seriously beginning to question the viability of a way of life that equates the acquisition of goods in the marketplace with happiness.

Scientific interest in psi is also growing. A large volume of research data has accumulated and it is becoming more difficult for skeptical scientists to avoid confrontations with their more adventurous colleagues. The "unexplained" variables in all sciences, previously cast aside in favor of more tangible investigation, are now being openly tackled by even those scientists who, out of great fear for jobs and reputations, were once "closet" psi researchers. In fact, the "secret life" of orthodox scientists would fill numerous volumes.

In Western culture, science has reigned supreme as a *method* of probing life's mysteries. We have been highly conditioned to feel comfortable with scientific explanation and to be impressed with scientific credentials as well. Now psi research, after its long, hard battle for official recognition, is becoming more respectable, and fashionable, and it is even possible for a scientist who is virtually unknown in his own specialty to emerge as a respected champion of psi. As long as *credentials* are apparent, our well-reinforced disposition is to increasingly view this kind of "defection from orthodoxy" as an important advance.

I am not proposing that we offhandedly reject scientific method, nor in any way deride its contribution to a greater public recognition and understanding of psi events. I am stressing that science should not be seen as a panacea for exploring alternative realities. At times, there is unfortunately a prevalent tendency to be cowed into exaggerating the scientific importance and validity of psi research in order to fend off overzealous critics. As we shall see, there are other equally valid ways of experiencing and giving meaning to life. I am, in part, referring to what psychologist Lawrence Le Shan has called "the clairvoyant reality."

While we cannot deal in depth here with the many profound implications of contemporary discoveries in physics and biology, it is increasingly apparent that the idea of an *objective out-there* world waiting to be analyzed by the *impartial* observer has been severely undermined. A view has been steadily evolving that sees Man as creator of his own relative, indeterminate, and therefore *subjective* experiences. Furthermore, in light of growing distaste for the illusory "good life" of the consumer society, scientific "progress" is often seen as detrimental to the emergence of new and more humanly satisfying dimensions of consciousness.

II

In this book, we shall be exploring one of mankind's great enigmas, the *aura*. For many, it is the vital key to a much greater and comprehensive understanding of psi events. Throughout history, there have been countless gifted individuals called "sensitives" or "psychics" who have provided definitions, theories, and descriptions of the aura. Science has repeatedly rejected this vast storehouse of "psychic" testimony because methods of producing this information have been unorthodox and generally seen as "impossible." People, for example, who claimed to have seen a luminous energy sphere around a human body have been highly suspect, especially if they also claimed the ability to diagnose illness by interpreting the colors and patterns of this mysterious emanation.

Scientific evidence was demanded. Without such proof, age-old claims would fall on deaf ears. When news of a Soviet technique perfected by Semyon Kirlian, capable of photographing energy patterns around plant leaves, small objects such as coins, and even human fingertips reached the West, many people felt that at last they would have proof that the aura was real.

Psychic Discoveries Behind the Iron Curtain, by Sheila Ostrander and Lynn Schroeder, provided the first widely distributed account of the Kirlian process. It helped to stimulate frenzied activity in American psi research circles. Almost immediately, attempts were made to duplicate the Kirlian system and scientifically validate Soviet claims. Did the photographs reveal the aura, an energy body more primary than the physical body? Could different states of mind influence the energy patterns? Did illness first manifest itself in this energy body, and could it be accurately diagnosed? Was this energy body our biological link with the universe?

It was hoped that the initial attempts to validate Soviet results would lead to even much greater discoveries. Important clues to psi events—the ability of mind to influence matter (psychokinesis), for example, and how a psychic healer's energy was transferred to beneficially affect another person's body—might possibly be found in the systematic study of this photographed energy.

Tens of thousands of Kirlian photographs were soon being taken all over the country. Diagrams of Kirlian devices and instructions were made available to amateurs as well. Newspapers and magazines that were usually flippant with, if not hostile to psi, commenced to bombard mass audiences with photographs of glowing energy patterns, often in kaleidoscopic color, around fingertips, coins of John F. Kennedy, and leaves.

Kirlian-mania was quickly becoming a sensational vehicle for attracting interest to virtually all aspects of the paranormal.

Over four years have passed since the publication of *Psychic Discoveries Behind the Iron Curtain*. Many conferences on psi phenomena, featuring discussions on the aura and Kirlian photography, have been held. It now appears that Kirlian-mania has reached its peak, and perhaps we can describe the more conservative attitude that is slowly emerging as not quite a letdown, but instead as a period of reflection and more sophisticated examination of what the past few years have produced.

Many researchers are debating whether Ostrander and Schroeder overdramatized their initial account of the aura and Kirlian photography. While their book often has been labeled a "popular" and "journalistic" appraisal of psi developments by those scientists who justifiably want to be cautious about evidence that may not have been rigorously gathered or inspected, the fact remains that many of these so-called "popular" accounts often appear to play a vital role in undermining the creaking conservatism that plagues all scientific progress.

Regardless of how the frenzy of the last four years may have time and again sacrificed quality for quantity, more scientists seem willing to explore psi in more comprehensive philosophical terms. More attempts are now being made to catalog the similarities to be found in the testimonies of "sensitives" and the statements of modern physicists.

The story of the aura is only beginning. The next phase will require a deeper understanding of these similarities, and a greater reluctance to uphold the validity of psi solely in scientific terms. As we shall discover, there are many important clues to be found in the work of early pioneers and in metaphysical and spiritual teachings. This book is dedicated to that aim.

NICHOLAS M. REGUSH

Montreal
June 1974

PROLOGUE

1.

PARACELSUS ON THE "VITAL FORCE" AND MEDICINE

Franz Hartmann

Controversial Theosophist and spiritualist, Franz Hartmann was a German-born doctor and member of the Order of the Temple of the Orient. The following selection is taken from his compilation of the works of sixteenth-century alchemist and physician, Philippus Theophrastus, Bombast of Honenheim, known as "Paracelsus."

Paracelsus believed that a vital force radiated within and around Man "like a luminous sphere." This force or magnetic influence, he said, could be used to heal and even made to act at a distance. A physician who was oblivious to this force, and who had no spiritual power, was described by Paracelsus as more than likely a quack. "If there were no teacher of medicine in the world," he once asked, "how would I set about to learn the art?" His reply was that he could learn "from the open book of nature."

While condemned as an eccentric—his work viewed as lunacy in the context of the Middle Ages—some of Paracelsus' vicious attacks on medicine, nevertheless, can be described today as inspiring. His writings provide, in many ways, a lucid and almost prophetic description of the machine-like quality of modern medical practice in an age of alienation and out-of-control technology.

My hope in presenting some of his thoughts at the outset of our study of the human aura, is to provide a critical tone, one which will enable us to understand that any developments at the frontiers of social thought inevitably meet with resistance. That the resistance will be overcome by one person's work is, of course, illusory. Contrary to public expectation, science does not readily incorporate new evidence and revolutionize its theory to fit the facts. Nor does scientific thinking develop in linear fashion, improving its theory and practice step by step. Rather, science appears bound to what Thomas S. Kuhn in The Structure of Scientific Revolution called "paradigms," universally preconceived models orienting the nature, scope and acceptability of scientific work. New ideas challenging these paradigms usually provoke strong criticisms and often extreme ridicule. Max Planck, quantum physics pioneer and Nobel Prize winner, once somewhat cryptically quipped that those opposing new ideas eventually die. When new paradigms finally emerge, they, in turn, dominate and resist further pretenders to the throne. The writings of Paracelsus, in this context thus provide an important spark and a "context" for later attempts to root out the many "invisibles" that have a profound impact on our lives. As psychic research continues to challenge the boundaries of the sciences, there will be a greater attempt to go back to earlier writings which have a bearing on modern theoretical structures. The work of Paracelsus provides one such example.

*   *   *

The practice of medicine is the art of restoring the sick to health. Modern medicine is, to a great extent, looked upon and employed as if it were a system by which man by his cunning and cleverness may cheat nature out of her dues and act against the laws of God with impunity, while, to many persons calling themselves physicians, it is merely a method of making money and gratifying their vanity.

Four hundred years ago Paracelsus spoke the following words to the physicians of his times, and we leave it to the reader to judge whether or not his words may find just application today. He says:

"You have entirely deserted the path indicated by nature, and built up an artificial system, which is fit for nothing but to swindle the public and to prey upon the pockets of the sick. Your safety is due to the fact that your gibberish is unintelligible to the public, who fancy that it must have a meaning, and the consequence is that no one can come near you without being cheated. Your art does not consist in curing the sick, but in worming yourself into the favour of the rich, in swindling the poor, and in gaining admittance to the kitchens of the noblemen of the country. You live upon imposture, and the aid and abetment of the legal profession enables you to carry on your impostures, and to evade punishment by the law. You poison the people and ruin their health; you are sworn to use diligence in your art, but how could you do so, as you possess no art, and all your boasted science is nothing but an invention to cheat and deceive? You denounce me because I do not follow your schools; but your schools can teach me nothing which would be worth knowing. You belong to the tribe of snakes, and I expect nothing but poison from you. You do not spare the sick: how could I expect that you would respect me, while I am cutting down your income by exposing your pretensions and ignorance to the public?"

There are three kingdoms acting in the constitution of man, an outer, an inner, and an innermost principle; namely, the external physical body; the inner (astral) man, and the innermost centre or God. Ordinary (regular) physicians know hardly anything about the external body; nothing about the inner man, the cause of the emotions, and less than nothing about God. Nevertheless, it is God who created and supports the inner man, and the outer form is the way in which the inner man is outwardly manifesting himself. Man's natural body is produced by nature; but the power in nature is God, and God is superior to nature. Man's divine spirit is therefore able to change his nature and to restore the health of his physical form.

The medicine of Paracelsus deals not merely with the external body of man, which belongs to the world of effects, but also with the inner man and with the world of causes; leaving never out of sight the universal presence of the divine cause of all things. It is therefore a holy science, and the practice of medicine a sacred mission, such as cannot be understood by those who are godless;

neither can divine power be conferred by diplomas and academical degrees. A physician who has no faith, and consequently no spiritual power in him, can be nothing else but an ignoramus and quack, even if he had graduated in all the medical colleges in the world and knew the contents of all the medical books that were ever written by man.

"The greatest and highest of all qualifications which a physician should possess is *Sapientia—i.e., Wisdom*—and without this qualification all his learning will amount to little or nothing as far as any benefit or usefulness to humanity is concerned.

"A physician should exercise his art—not for his own sake—but for the sake of the patient; if he practises merely for his own benefit, such a physician resembles a wolf, and is even worse than an ordinary murderer; for while a man may defend himself against a murderous attack made upon him upon the highroad, he has no means of defence against the murderer who, under the guise of a benefactor and protected by law, comes to steal his goods and destroy his life.

"He should also be well experienced; for there are many kinds of disease and they cannot be known without experience and learning. No one ever knows so much that he could not learn more. Every art requires experience. You cannot become a good painter, sculptor, or shoemaker by the mere reading of books, much less can you be a good physician without being experienced. He should know the laws of nature, but above all the constitution of man, the invisible no less than the visible one. His knowledge will strengthen his faith, and his faith will endow him with power, so that he will be like an apostle, healing the sick, the blind, and the halt."

The medicine of Paracelsus therefore rests upon four pillars, which are: 1. *Philosophy, i.e.,* a knowledge of physical nature; 2, *Astronomy, i.e.,* a knowledge of the powers of the mind; 3, *Alchemy, i.e.,* a knowledge of the divine powers in man, and 4, *The personal virtue* (holiness) *of the physician.*

1. A physician should be a philosopher, *i.e.*, acquainted with the laws of external nature.

"The knowledge of nature is the foundation of the science of medicine, and it is taught by the four great departments of science: *Philosophy, Astronomy, Alchemy*, and *Physical Science*. These four sciences cover a large field, and require a great deal of study.

"A physician must be a *Philosopher*; that is to say, he must dare to use his own reason and not cling to antiquated opinions and book-authorities. He must above all be in possession of that faculty which is called Intuition, and which cannot be acquired by blindly following the footsteps of another; he must be able to see his own way. There are natural philosophers and there are artificial philosophers. The former have a knowledge of their own; the latter have borrowed knowledge from their books.

"He who wants to know man must look upon him as a whole and not as a patched-up piece of work. If he finds a part of the human body diseased, he must look for the causes which produce the disease, and not merely treat the external effects. Philosophy—*i.e.*, the true perception and understanding of cause and effect—is the mother of the physician, and explains the origin of all his diseases.

"A physician who knows nothing more about his patient than what the latter will tell him knows very little indeed. He must be able to judge from the external appearance of the latter about his internal condition. He must be able to see the internal in the external man; for if he wanted to experiment merely according to his own fancy the world could not furnish him enough patients to arrive at the end of his experiments."

"Nature—not man—is the physician. Man has lost the true light of reason, and the animal intellect with its speculations and theories has usurped the place. Try to enable yourself to follow nature again, and she will be your instructor. Learn to know the storehouse of nature and the boxes in which her virtues are stored up. The ways of nature are simple and she does not require any complicated prescriptions."

2. "A physician must be an *Astronomer*, for he ought to know the influences of the seasons, of heat and cold, of dryness and moisture, of light and darkness, etc., upon the organism of man. There is a time for everything and what may be good at one time, may be evil at another. There is a time for rain and a time when the roses are blooming, and it is not sufficient that a physician should be able to judge about today, he should also know what tomorrow will bring."

Man's body is itself a product of mind and its condition depends to a great extent on the state of his mind. All his diseases in so far as they are not directly due to external mechanical causes, are due to mental conditions.

"Astronomy is the upper part of philosophy by which the whole of the microcosm may become known. Philosophy deals with the elements of earth and water, belonging to man's constitution; Astronomy deals with his air and fire (the mind.) There is a heaven and earth in man as there is in the macrocosm, and in that heaven there are all the celestial influences, whose visible representations we see in the sky, such as the planets and stars, the Milky Way, the Zodiac, etc.

"The terrestrial part of man is a child of the earth, and the astral man is a child of the astral world, and as the two worlds are intimately connected with each other, the physician should be acquainted with the influences of the astral as well as with those of the terrestrial world. Man's diseases do not originate in himself; they originate from the influences which act upon him and enter his constitution. The astral influences are invisible, but they act upon man, unless he knows how to protect himself against them. Heat and light are intangible and incorporeal; nevertheless, they act upon man, and the same takes place with other invisible influences. If the air becomes vitiated, it may poison man's body; if the astral influences are in a state of corruption, they may do likewise. The elements themselves are invisible; that which is visible belongs merely to the external form. The Arcanum of Man—*i.e.*, the real inner man, is invisible; that which we see of him is not an essential part of his constitution, but merely his external corporeal form.

"The things which we see are not the active principles, but merely the *corpus* containing them; the visible forms are merely external expressions of invisible principles. Forms are, so to say, the vehicles of powers, and they may be visible or invisible. The invisible air and the ether of space, or a perfectly clear and, therefore, invisible crystal, are just as much corporeal as the solid earth, a piece of wood, or a rock. Each of these corporeal things has its own particular life and inhabitants; we walk about in the air, although the air is corporeal, fishes swim about in the water, and the yolk of an egg rests in the albumen without sinking to the bottom of the shell. The yolk represents the Earth, and the white represents the invisible surroundings of the Earth, and the invisible part acts upon the visible one, but only the philosopher perceives the way in which that action takes place."

3. "He should be an *Alchemist*; that is to say, he should understand the *Chemistry of Life*. Medicine is not merely a science, but an art; it does not consist merely in compounding pills and plasters and drugs of all kinds; but it deals with the processes of life which must be understood before they can be guided. All art, all wisdom, all power, acts from one centre towards the periphery of the circle, and whatever is enclosed within the circle may be regarded as medicine. A powerful will may cure where doubt will end in a failure. The character of the physician may act more powerfully upon the patient than all the drugs employed.

"The psychical surroundings of the patient may have a great influence upon the course of his disease. If he is waited upon by persons who are in sympathy with him, it will be far better for him, than if his wife or his attendants wish for his death. In a case of sickness, the patient, the physician, and the attendants should be—so to say—all one heart and one soul."

4. The physician must have the *natural qualification* for his occupation.

"He who can cure disease is a physician. To cure diseases is an art which cannot be acquired by the mere reading of books, but which must be learned by experience. Neither emperors nor popes, neither colleges nor high schools can create physicians. They can confer privileges and cause a person who is not a physician to appear as if he were one; but they cannot cause him to be what he is not; they can give him permission to kill, but they cannot enable him to cure the sick, if he has not already been ordained by God. Theory should precede practice; but if it consists in mere suppositions and assumptions, and is not confirmed by practical works, such a theory is worthless and ought to be abandoned.

"One of the most necessary requirements for a physician is perfect purity and singleness of purpose. He should be free of ambition, vanity, envy, unchastity, pomposity, and self-conceit, because these vices are the outcome of ignorance and incompatible with the light of divine wisdom which should illuminate the mind of the true physician; but our practitioners of medicine will not believe me when I say that it is necessary that a physician to be successful should be virtuous; because they imagine that success is due only to learning and they cannot realize that all true wisdom and power is derived from God."

All organic functions are caused by the activity of one universal principle of Life. This principle acts in all the members of the body, either slow or quick, perceptible or imperceptible, consciously or unconsciously, normal or abnormal, according to the constitution of the organs in which it is active. As long as the character (the spirit) of an entity is preserved, it acts in that entity as a whole; if the form is broken up and loses its character, it manifests itself in other forms; the life which is active in a man during his lifetime in causing the organic functions of his body, will manifest its activity in creating worms in his body after the spirit has left the form. The spirit is the centre which attacts the principle of life; if the spirit has left the form, life will be attracted to other centres.

If the activity of the life principle takes place in a form in a normal and regular manner, unimpeded by any obstacles, such a state is called health. If its activity is impeded by some cause, and it if acts abnormally or irregularly, such a state is called "disease."

This principle of life is called by Paracelsus, Archaeus. It is not a material substance, in the usual acceptation of that term, but a spiritual essence, everywhere present and invisible. It may cause or cure disease according to the conditions under which it acts, as it may be pure or impure, healthy or poisoned by other influences. The animal organism attracts it from its surroundings and from the nutriments which enter into its form; it may assimilate it, and lose it again. "The Archaeus, or Liquor Vitae," constitutes the invisible man. The invisible man is hidden in the visible one, and is formed in the shape of the outer one as long as it remains in that outer one. The inner man is, so to say, the shadow or the counterpart of the material body. It is ethereal in its nature, still it is substance: it directs the growth and the formation and dissolution of the form in which it is contained; it is the noblest part in physical man. As a man's picture is reflected in a mirror, so the form of the physical man is reflected in the invisible body.

"The Archaeus is an essence that is equally distributed in all parts of the human body, if the latter is in a healthy condition; it is the invisible nutriment from which the visible body draws its strength, and the qualities of each of its parts correspond to the nature of the physical parts that contain it.

"All diseases, except such as come from mechanical causes, have an invisible origin, and of such sources popular medicine knows very little. Men who are devoid of the power of spiritual perception are unable to recognize the existence of anything that cannot be seen externally. Popular medicine knows therefore next to nothing about any diseases that are not caused by mechanical

means, and the science of curing internal diseases consists almost entirely in the removal of causes that have
produced some mechanical obstruction. But the number
of diseases that originate from some unknown causes is
far greater than those that come from mechanical causes,
and for such diseases our physicians know no cure, because not knowing such causes they cannot remove them.
All they can prudently do is to observe the patient and
make their guesses about his condition; and the patient
may rest satisfied if the medicines administered to him do
him no serious harm, and do not prevent his recovery.
The best of our popular physicians are the ones that do
the least harm. But, unfortunately, some poison their
patients with mercury, others purge them or bleed them
to death. There are some who have learned so much that
their learning has driven out all their common sense, and
there are others who care a great deal more for their own
profit than for the health of their patients. A disease does
not change its state to accommodate itself to the knowledge of the physician, but the physician should be a
servant of Nature, and not her enemy; he should be able
to guide and direct her in her struggle for life, and not
throw, by his unreasonable interference, fresh obstacles
in the way of recovery."

Part One

The Pioneer Work

2.

PRINCIPLES

Franz Anton Mesmer

According to Franz Anton Mesmer, a Viennese doctor, "Everything in the universe is contiguous by means of a universal fluid in which all bodies are immersed." The idea that a life-sustaining vital force is present in all organisms certainly did not originate with Mesmer. The medieval physician Paracelsus, for example, believed, "The vital force is not enclosed in man but radiates within and around him like a luminous sphere." This force or magnetic influence, he said, could be used to heal and even made to act at a distance.

But it was Mesmer who ushered in a new period of interest in magnetism. He believed that the elasticity, fluidity, and movement of the body could be stimulated by this force. Someone well endowed with this energy could learn to safely transfer it to another human being. He anticipated a storm of criticism when, in 1775, he wrote in his foreword to his Dissertation on the Discovery of Animal Magnetism: *"I am well aware that this little work raises many difficulties, but it must be borne in mind that they are of such a nature as not to be solved by any amount of reasoning without the assistance of experience."*

Dressed in silk robes, a wand in his hand, Mesmer officiated at his plush clinic while people stepped into the baquet—*a great tub containing water, iron filings, and other mysterious ingredients. It wasn't surprising that in 1784 a commission led by Benjamin Franklin branded him*

11

a quack. Paracelsus, too, had been accused of being a charlatan in his time.

Interest in psi and especially in the aura has revived Mesmer's often crude but sometimes extremely sophisticated view of man's intimate relationship to the universe. In the following selection, translated by Jerome Eden, Mesmer states some of his basic principles. One of Eden's main interests has been to emphasize Mesmer's great contribution to the idea that a life energy exists. I have marked with asterisks some of the more important principles that have, as we shall see, an important bearing on recent aura research and speculation.

* * *

*God exists as an uncreated source; in nature two created sources exist: matter and movement.

*Primary matter [i.e. energy] is that which has been employed by the Creator for the formation of all beings.

Movement brings about the development of all possibilities.

We have not yet formed a positive idea of the primary matter; it is placed between the simple being [i.e., act of creation] and the beginning of the composed being: It is like unity with regard to arithmetic quantities.

*Impenetrability constitutes the essence of primary matter; impenetrability belongs to it alone, and to none other.

Matter is indifferent to being in movement or in repose.

*Matter in movement constitutes fluidity; the cessation of movement in matter produces solidity.

If two or more parts of matter are in repose, a combination results from this state.

The condition of the combination is a condition relative to the movement or repose of matter.

Only in these relations is found the source of all possible variations, in forms and in properties.

Since matter is capable only of different combinations, ideas that we have concerning numbers or arithmetic quantities can serve to make us aware of the immensity of developmental possibilities.

Considering the particles of the elementary matter as units, one can easily realize that these units can assemble themselves by twos, by threes, by fours, fives, etc., and that such assemblages will result in sums or aggregates which can be continued to infinity.

The manner of assemblage of these units into aggregates constitutes the first species of possible combinations.

Considering then these first combinations as new units, we will have as many species of units as there will be numbers possible, and we will be able to conceive also of assemblages of these units among themselves.

If these assemblages or aggregates are formed of units of the same species, they constitute the whole of *homogeneous matter*.

If these aggregates are formed of units of different species, they constitute the whole of *heterogeneous matter*.

From these diverse combinations, by which each can proceed to infinity, one can conceive of the immensity of all possible combinations.

Properly speaking, the elementary matter does not have, by itself, any property. It is indifferent to being in any type of combination; and all properties which it presents to us are the result or product of its diverse combinations.

*The whole of a quantity of matter, which becomes and is regarded as forming a combined entity, is that which we call a *body*.

*If in the combination of the constituent parts of a body, there exists an order, in consequence of which there results new effects, or new combinations, such a unit is called an *organic body*.

*If the parts of matter are combined in such an order, from which there results no new effect, or new combination, the resultant unit is called an *inorganic body*.

*What we call an *inorganic body* is purely a metaphysical distinction, because if there were absolutely no effect of a body, it would not exist.

The elementary matter of all the constituent parts of bodies is of the same nature. This identity is proven in the final dissolution of bodies.

If we consider the constituent parts of bodies as existences, separate from one another, we have the idea of *locality*.

Locations are imaginary points in which matter is found or can be found.

The quantity of these imaginary points determines the idea of *space*.

If the matter changes location, and occupies successively different points, this change or this action of matter is what we call *movement*.

Movement modifies matter.

*The first movement is an immediate effect of creation, and this movement supplied to the matter is the sole cause of all the different combinations and all the forms which exist.

*This movement is constantly and universally maintained by the most tenuous parts of the matter which we call *fluid*.

We shall consider three things in all movements of the fluid matter: the *direction*, the *speed*, and the *tone*.

The tone is the kind or mode of movement which maintains its material parts in a specific condition.

There are only two directions, and these are directly opposed, one to the other. All other directions are composed of these two; by one of these directions the parts approach each other, and by the other they diverge. Combination occurs through the one; the other results in dissolution.

Equality in the force of these two directions causes the parts neither to approach nor to diverge from each other; consequently they are neither in the state of cohesion nor dissolution, but are in the state which constitutes perfect fluidity.

To the extent that the two directions diverge from the state of equality, the fluidity diminishes and solidity increases, and *vice versa*.

Combination or primary cohesion takes place when the

directions of movement of the parts happen to oppose one another, or when their speed toward the same direction is unequal.

A quantity of matter in the state of cohesion or of rest, constitutes the solidity or the mass of bodies.

The first impulse to movement which the matter has received in an absolutely filled space, is sufficient to give it all the directions and all the gradations of speed possible.

Matter conserves the quantity of movement that it has received initially.

The different kinds of movement can be considered either in the entire body, or in the constituent parts.

The constituent parts of the fluid matter can be combined in all possible ways, and can receive all kinds of movement possible among themselves.

All the properties may be organized or unorganized, depending upon the manner in which their parts are combined, and the movement of these parts among themselves.

If a quantity of fluid is set in motion in one direction, that is called a *current*.

If we suppose a current which insinuates itself into a body, dividing itself into an infinite number of small currents, infinitely tenuous, in a pattern of lines, we call these subdivisions *streams*.

When the elementary matter, either by moving in opposing directions, or at unequal speeds, sets itself at rest, and thereby acquires some cohesion, from the way in which the particles are combined there result some spaces or *interstices*.

The interstices of masses remain permeable to the currents or streams of the subtle matter.

All bodies submerged in a fluid are obedient to the movement of that fluid.

It follows that if a body is submerged in a current, it is drawn along in its direction, which does not happen to a body obeying several mixed directions.

*Considering that all is one whole, there cannot exist an incoming current without an outgoing current, and *vice versa*.

*Within the universe there exists a fixed, uniform, and constant amount of movement, which was impressed upon matter in the beginning.

This impression of movement was made upon one mass of fluid at first, so that all the contiguous parts of fluid have received the same impressions.

It resulted in two opposed directions, and in all the progressions of other composed movements.

Given (A) (B), all being one whole, if A moves towards B, it may mean two things: that B was displaced by A, and A was replaced by B.

This figure explains: 1. All the gradations and directions of movement. 2. A movement of universal and particular rotation. 3. This movement is only propagated for a certain distance from the first impression. 4. That currents, both universal and particular, are more or less composed.

By means of these currents, the sum of movement is distributed and applied to all parts of matter.

There exists within the modification of the currents, the source of all the combinations and of all the movements possible, developed and to be developed. Thus in the infinite number of combinations of matter, as the movement of one or another type may have brought about by chance, those combinations which might be considered perfect (that is to say, where there is no degree of contradiction of movement), have subsisted and are conserved, and in perfecting themselves, have succeeded in forming the matrices for the propagation of the species. One can gain an idea of this operation by comparing it with crystallizations.

*All bodies are floating in a current of the subtle matter (i.e., *universal fluid*).

Thus it is that by the opposition of directions, and unequal speeds, the particles touch each other. They are left thereby without movement, and form the first degree of cohesion. An infinity of molecules more gross are induced and applied more extensively to the first (cohesed particle) all of which are at rest, and constitute a mass which becomes the germ and origin of all large bodies.

Two particles which are attracted constitute an obstacle to the two streams of currents which correspond to them. Being unable to pass with integrity, these two streams join together with two adjacent streams, and accelerate their movement, and this acceleration is due to the passages or interstices (of the particles) being more restricted.

Upon approaching a solid body, every current is accelerated, and this acceleration occurs by virtue of the compactibility or solidity of the matter.

These streams either retain or lose their initial direction in passing, and thus their parts may follow a confused movement.

If this current, in traversing a body, is split into two separate streams, and if the opposing fibres (of the body) split in two, the streams insinuate themselves mutually into the interstices of each, without disturbing their motion; the result is apparent attraction, or the phenomenon of the magnet.

If instead of insinuating themselves, the streams collide so that one predominates over the other, the result is repulsion.

Equilibrium demands that when a current enters into a body, another equal to it flows out of it, and yet the movement of the departing streams may be weaker, because they are divergent and scattered.

The nature of the universal and particular streams being thus determined, one can account for the origin and progress of celestial bodies.

The coarsest molecule which chance has formed, let us say, has become the center of a particular current.

The current, in proportion to its involvement of the floating molecule which it surrounds, has enlarged this central body. Thus the current becomes accelerated and more all-encompassing, taking to itself coarser matter. This action is extended to a distance where the current finds itself counter-balanced by the similar action from another central body.

As the action is produced equally from the periphery to the center, the bodies necessarily become *spheres*.

The difference of their mass depends upon the random combination of the first molecules, which gives them greater or lesser size.

The differences of their mass corresponds to the extent of the space which is found between them.

As all matter has received a movement of rotation, there results in each central body a movement upon its axis.

As these bodies are relatively eccentric to the whirlpool in which they are rotating, they move away from the center up to the point where the centrifugal movement is proportionate to the force of the current which carries them towards the center.

All celestial bodies have a reciprocal tendency towards each other, in proportion to their mass and distance: this action is most directly exercised between the points of their surfaces which face each other.

These spherical bodies turning upon their axes, and reciprocally exposing to each other one half of their surfaces, receive mutual impressions upon that half. These mutual and alternative impressions constitute the flux and reflux in each of their spheres.

These actions, and these reciprocally described relationships constitute the influence between all celestial bodies. They are manifested in more remote bodies by the effects which they produce upon each other. They disturb one another in their revolutions; they arrest, retard, or accelerate the movement of each other's orbits.

*Hence there is a constant law in nature, that there is a mutual influence upon the totality of bodies, and consequently this influence exerts itself upon all the constituent parts and their properties.

*This reciprocal influence and the relations of all co-existent bodies, form what is called *magnetism*.

3.

OD

Baron Karl Von Reichenbach

In 1845 Baron Karl Von Reichenbach, a German industrialist and scientist, added another chapter to the belief in the existence of a universal energy. Facing mechanistic nineteenth-century scientific views, he too became frustrated and impatient with the hostility his ideas encountered and he eventually resolved to take his case to the laymen in the form of popularly written letters.

He begins his controversial Letters on Od and Magnetism *by asking a number of intriguing questions. Why is it that there are some people who have a great aversion to the color yellow and generally no one with a distaste for blue? Why do some people have painful impressions when looking at mirrors? Why do some people only have a good night's sleep when lying on their right sides? Some people hate crowds and refuse to sit between others. Some people have an aversion to silverware, to hot, rich, and overcooked food, and to heat from an iron stove. Why?*

Reichenbach's attempt to answer these questions ranks with the very best of detective work and he arrives at the conclusion that all *these peculiarities affect a certain group of people he calls "sensitives." "Their sufferings," he writes, "are the consequence of their hitherto unrecognized peculiarity in the sensory faculty. . . ."*

In this selection we follow some of Reichenbach's ingenious research work with sensitives as he attempts to demonstrate that "od" is a universal energy felt more acutely by sensitives and existing in varying degrees of concentration, penetrating everything.

* * *'

Just procure a natural crystal, as big a one as you can get, say a gypsum spar two spans in length, a heavy spar, or a St. Gothard mountain-crystal a foot long, and lay it horizontally over the corner of a table or the arm of a chair, so that both ends project unsupported. Now lead a "sensitive" person up to it, and tell him to put the palm of his left hand within three, four, or six inches distance from each end of the crystal, one end after the other; it will not be half a minute before he will tell you that a fine, cool current is coming against his hand from the end of the upper part of the peak of the crystal, while from the other end—but on the lower, broken surface, that on which the crystal grew—a certain feeling of lukewarmness reaches his hand. He will find the feeling of coolness pleasant and refreshing, that of the lukewarmness unpleasant, and accompanied by a disagreeable feeling, one almost of disgust, which, after a short period, will affect his whole arm, if kept there, and produce a sort of feeling of lassitude.

When I first made this observation, it was just as novel as puzzling; nobody, wherever I went, would believe it. Meantime I have repeated it with hundreds of sensitives in Vienna; it has been confirmed in England, Scotland, and France; and anyone can easily put it to the proof himself, as sensitives exist everywhere. When they hold their hand near other parts of the crystal, say the bevelments on each side, they do, it is true, feel the two sensations of coolness and lukewarmness, but to an incomparably weaker degree than at the two ends, which are opposite poles. Non-sensitives feel nothing at all.

As these contrasting sensations are excited without the crystal being touched, and at a distance of several inches—in fact, in the case of strongly sensitive persons at a distance of several feet—it seemed to be that from these so-to-speak semi-organic stones something was proceeding, emanating, radiating, something as yet unknown to natural science, something which, however incapable we may be of seeing it, still makes its existence known through its effects upon the body. Now sensitives being, so far as *feeling* is concerned, so very much more capable than other men, the thought occurred to me that they might, in certain respects, be superior to us also in *the sense of sight*, and perhaps be able, in dense darkness, to perceive something of these peculiar emanations from crystals.

To put this to the proof, one dark night in May 1844 I took an immensely large mountain-crystal with me on a visit to a highly sensitive girl, Miss Angelica Sturmann; her doctor, Professor Lippich, a man celebrated as a pathologist, was present on the occasion. We put two rooms into complete darkness, and in one of them I placed the crystal, in a spot unknown to the others. After pausing a little, to allow our eyes to get accustomed to the dark, we brought the girl into the room where the crystal was. Only a short time elapsed before she told me the place where I had set it down. The whole body of the crystal, she said, was glowing through and through with a fine light, while a body of blue light, the size of one's hand, was streaming out of its peak, in constant motion to and fro, and occasionally emitting sparks; it was tulip-shaped, and disappearing in fine vapour at the summit.

When I turned the crystal round, she saw a dense red and yellow smoke rising over the butt-end. You can imagine how delighted I was with this statement. It was the first observation of thousands of others similar to it, which followed on from that day to this, made with crystals under innumerable variations of conditions, observations which, through the medium of a multitude of sensitive persons, established the fact that the phenomena produced by crystals to the sense of touch are accompanied by phenomena to the sense of vision, the latter phenomena following the former *pari passu*, in polar contrast of blue and red-yellow, and only perceptible by sensitives.

If you wish to make these experiments for yourself, I must warn you that you can only expect them to succeed in *absolute darkness*. The crystalline light is so fine and so extremely weak that if so much as a trace of any other light is perceptible anywhere in the dark chamber, it is sufficient to blind the sensitive observer, that is, to temporarily blunt his excitability of sense for so extremely weak a degree of light. Furthermore, there are but few human beings so highly sensitive to be able, like the young lady I have named, to perceive this delicate light after so short a period of darkness. For sensitives of a middling degree of power it has mostly taken one to two hours in the dark to sufficiently relieve their eyesight from the over-excitation of day- or lamp-light, and thus adequately to prepare it for the detection of the crystal-light. I have even had several cases in which weak sensitives gave no result after three hours, but who nevertheless succeeded quite well during the fourth hour in seeing crystals give out light and in convincing themselves of the reality of the phenomenon.

Now you are impatient to know what this really means, and where these phenomena fit in to physics and physiology, both as to their subjective and objective particulars. They are not heat, although they excite similar sensations to those of lukewarmness and coolness; there is no conceivable source of heat in the case, and, were there any, it would be perceived, not only by sensitives, but also by non-sensitives, or in the ultimate issue by a fine thermoscope. They are not electricity; for there is no excitation present to account for the eternally flowing stream, the electroscope is not affected, and conduction, in accordance with the laws of electricity, is without effect. It cannot be magnetism and diamagnetism, because crystals are not magnetic, and diamagnetism does not take effect in all crystals in the same sense, but in widely differing and contrasted senses—a matter that has no place here at all. It cannot be ordinary light, because, although light is here as an accompaniment, mere light never produces sensations of lukewarmness and coolness, etc.

Well, then, after saying all that, what *are* the

phenomena you have described? If you really wish to know, you compel me to admit that I do not know myself. I am becoming aware through sundry avenues of the presence of a natural force, for which I am unable to find a place on the record established by those forces we already know of. If my judgment of the facts I have been able to gather has not gone astray, this force fits in between electricity, magnetism, and heat, without being identifiable with any of the three; so, in the embarrassment created by the occasion, I have provisionally designated it by the word "od."

Sensitives you now know, and the element in which they move you know, namely, that force of nature which I have designated by the word "od." But with all that we have only lifted one corner of the hem of the great odic garment in which the universe has wrapped itself. That remarkable force of od streams not only from the poles of the crystal, but gushes also from numerous other sources in the great world of being just as strongly, and even more strongly still.

First and foremost I shall take you to the stars, and, in fact, to the sun itself. Post a sensitive person in the shade, give him an ordinary unfilled barometer-tube, or any other sort of glass rod, or even a wooden stick, in his left hand, and let him hold the rod in the sunshine, while his person and hand remain in the shade. You will shortly learn something from this simple experiment that will surprise you. You naturally expect that the person experimenting will perhaps feel the rod getting warm; the most that can happen will surely be that the sunshine will warm it up.

But you will hear exactly the opposite: the sensitive's hand will feel a number of effects, but the sum-total of them all will be—a coolness. If such a hand withdraws the rod into the shade, the coolness will vanish, and the hand will feel the rod getting warm; if it puts the rod back into the sunshine, the rod will once more grow cool to its sensory perception; it can check the correctness of its own sensations by continuing to change about from one position to the other.

There are consequently some very simple, but so far unobserved, factors in existence under the influence of which the direct sunbeam not only does not warm, but, in a most unexpected and unusual manner, cools. And as to this coolness, sensitives will tell you that it bears every resemblance in its effects to those exercised by the coolness felt from the upper peak of the mountain-crystal.

Now, if this coolness is something in the nature of od, it will necessarily find some expression in the dark as a phenomenon of light. You will succeed in finding this out if you will perform one of my experiments as follows: I hung a copper wire so as to go from a fully lighted room into the darkness of the *camera obscura*. Then I put the end of the wire out into the sunshine. Scarcely was this done when the part of the wire that was in the dark began to get luminous, and a small, flamelike phenomenon, the size of a finger, rose up at its extremity. The sunshine consequently infused an odic element into the wire, seen by sensitives streaming out in the darkness under the form of light.

But take one step further; let the sunbeam fall on a good glass prism, and throw the colours of the rainbow onto the nearest wall. Let the sensitive person with the glass rod in his left hand try the colours one after the other. If he holds it so as to catch only the blue or violet colour in the air, the sensation that this will excite in him will be one of a highly agreeable coolness, much purer and cooler than that which occurred with the unrefracted sunbeam. If, instead of this, he puts the rod into the yellow ray, or, better still, into the red ray, the comfortable feeling of coolness will vanish on the instant, and be replaced by one of heat; a disagreeable lukewarmness will make his whole arm heavy.

You can make the sensitive hold a bare finger on the colours, instead of using the rod as intermediary; the effect will be the same; I only devised the rod for the purpose of shutting off the actual heat rays from his hand by means of a bad conductor of heat. These effects of refracted sunlight will be found exactly similar to those of the poles of the crystal. Hence you see: od exercising both kinds of effect is contained in the sunbeam; it streams towards us from our star of day every moment in immeasurable floods, along with the light and heat, and forms a newly discovered mighty solar agent, the extent of whose functions we have no present means of estimating. [*Here Reichenbach refers back to his observation in a previous letter that some people have an aversion to the color yellow while not to blue. N. M. R.*]

Have we not seen that the pole of the crystal that breathed forth an agreeable coolness was one that emitted blue light? And do we not here, by quite a different route, come upon sunlight distributing with its blue ray an extremely agreeable and refreshing coolness? And, vice versa, had not the red-yellow light of the other pole of the crystal, and also the red-yellow ray of the sun, produced feelings of nausea and discomfort in the sensitives? You see how in two cases, standing so infinitely wide apart, blue had invariably for its sequel sensations of comfort, and red-yellow feelings of discomfort. Herewith you receive a preliminary hint to put you on your guard against all rash judgment of sensitive persons in the matter of their alleged whims. You see that, in fact, something more must lie hidden in the yellow and blue of our colours than their mere optical effect on the retina of the eye, that here a deep-down, instinctive sense of a subtle, unknown *something* guides the feeling and intuitive judgment of our sensitives, and that this is a matter worth the utmost efforts of our powers of observation.

Now, leaving colours on one side, I wish to arm you with one more easy experiment that I have often made for isolating the odic content of sunbeams. Polarize them in the ordinary way, so that they fall at an angle of 35° on a bundle of a dozen panes of glass. Then let the sensitive observer hold the rod in his left hand now in the reflected light and now in the light that has passed through. You will always hear that the former sends odic cool and the latter odic mawkishness along the rod to the sense of feeling in the hand.

If you are in the mood, you can take a little rise out of the chemists in this connection. Get two similar glasses of water and put one standing in the reflected and the other in the filtered sunlight. After they have been there six to eight minutes, let a sensitive sip from them. He will tell you at once that the water taken out of the reflected light tastes cool and slightly acidulous, and that the water taken out of the filtered light tastes mawkish and somewhat bitter. Do something more: put a small glass vessel filled with water in the blue light of the spectrum, and another one in the orange; or put one of them at the pointed end of a large mountain-crystal, and the other at the butt-end. In all these cases you may be sure that the sensitive will find the water that has been in the blue light pleasant, and lightly acidulated, and that which has been in the orange nauseating, rather bitter, and crude. He will drink the first glass off with pleasure, if you let him do so; but, if you force him into drinking the other, an event may betide you that happened once to myself, namely, that the sensitive shortly afterwards had a violent fit of vomiting. Now give the water to the gentlemen of the analytical profession, and ask them to try out the elements of the "amarum" and the "acidum" from it.

Proceed with the moonlight as you have done with the sunlight. You will obtain similar, but in part polarically contrasted results. A glass rod held by a sensitive's left hand in full, pure moonlight will not yield him coolness, but lukewarmness. A glass of water that has been sometime in the moonlight he will find tasting more insipid and mawkish than another that has been standing a moderate time in the shade. Everyone knows the great influence the moon has on many people; all persons subject to its influence are without exception sensitives, and as a rule pretty keenly sensitive. And, as the moon demonstrably exercises odic effects, while its influence on lunatic patients corresponds exactly with the effects that can

be produced through other odic sources, it is as an od-
distributive star of great importance for us.

The element of odic force is thus radiated towards us
so abundantly by sunlight and moonlight that we can lay
hold of it at our ease and make use of it in simple experiments. How unbounded its influence is on the whole of
humanity, and even on the whole animal and vegetable
kingdom, will be proved shortly. Od is, accordingly, a
cosmic force that radiates from star to star, and has the
whole universe for its field, just like light and heat.

You have seen that, if I laid my right hand in the left of
a sensitive, an agreeably cool feeling was aroused, but
that, if I did the same with my left, a disagreeable warmth
and sensation of nausea was the result. The procedure
can be reversed: lay your own left hand in the sensitive's
right, and he will experience a cool and agreeable sensation; put your own right hand in his, and the disagreeable, lukewarm sensation will commence. This gives us a
law: contact of hands odically like (left with left, or right
with right) is disagreeably lukewarm; contact of hands
odically unlike (left with right) is agreeably cool.

[*Reichenbach refers here to the remark he made in his first
letter "to the effect that there were people who found it disagreeable to be given a man's hand, and who wrenched themselves free
if the hand they extended was retained. According to common
custom, men always give each other their right hands, and thus
cause a contact of hands odically like; such a contact is disagreeably lukewarm to sensitives, becomes quite penal, then speedily
unendurable, and—they free themselves." N. M. R.*]

Go a step further: put the fingers of your right hand on
the sensitive's left arm, on his shoulder, under his armpit,
on his temples, on the small of his back, on his knee, his
foot, his toes, everywhere on the left side of the sensitive's
body, and he will feel them, your right fingers, cool and
comfortable: the contacts are all odically unlike. Do the
same to the sensitive's right side with the fingers of your
left, and they will produce the same feelings of coolness:
those are unlike contacts too. But do all these touches on

the sensitive's left side with the fingers of your left hand, or on his right side with the fingers of your right, and it will all be found nauseating and, every touch, disagreeable: they are like contacts.

Put my data to the proof by another kind of pairing taken from common life. Stand as close to a sensitive as soldiers do when drawn up in rank and file; the whole of your right side will then touch the whole of the sensitive's left: you will hear no complaint from him on the subject. But now make a right-about turn, so as to bring your left side into contact with the sensitive's left, and complaints will at once be forthcoming: he will have a sickening sense of discomfort, and if you do not turn round again soon, he will not keep on, but will take a step backwards. In the first instance an unlike, in the second a like, contact was at work.

Choose another condition. Post yourself close behind your sensitive, with your front to his rear; or in the same way, in front of him, with your rear to his front. In both cases your right side is planted against the sensitive's right, and your left against his left. In both respects these are odically like pairings; the sensitive cannot endure them, and if you do not speedily change the situation, he will change it for you by stepping to one side. [*Reichenbach refers here to his first letter "where I drew your attention to the fact that there were some people who could not bear others standing before them or behind them, and on that account avoided popular assemblies, crowds, and marketplaces. You see now what good grounds they had for their action." N. M. R.*]

I know strong and active young men who do not like riding. It seems something almost against human nature: to youthful vigour it is surely the height of enjoyment to be tossed up on horseback. But when one is in the saddle one has to present like sides to those of one's mount. The case is thus exactly the same as having a man's back immediately in front of one. The men I found exhibiting this disinclination were all sensitives.

In the same way there are women who cannot give a

child a ride on their back, not even for a few minutes for pure sport. The case is almost the same as the foregoing; it comes to the same as having someone close behind one; women of this sort are always sensitives.

Many men are simply unable to sleep two in a bed; *mauvais çoucheurs*—bad bedfellows—are proverbial. The reason breaks in upon us after what we have discussed.

But the practice common to all civilized societies of presenting our right side to all privileged persons, by always standing to their left, sitting down at their left, taking their left arm, has its fundamental cause in our odic nature. It is said, of course, that this is to leave the privileged person's right hand free. That may play its part in regard to the custom, but the influence of sensitivity must bear down the scale with still greater weight. When two men sit side by side they set free their od mutually upon each other; the man on the right gets a discharge of negative od from the man on the left, the man on the left positive od from the man on his right. The right-hand-side man thus gains as much in negativity as the left-hand-side man loses, and the latter gains as much in positivity as the man on the right discharges. Now the condition of greater odic negativity, as we know, is the colder and more agreeable of the two, and that of greater positivity the warmer and more disagreeable. So when we place a lady on our right, she acquires just as much comfort as the man on her left takes upon himself in the way of discomfort. The key to this ancient custom, therefore, is not to be found entirely in tradition, but rather in the innermost depth of human nature. The matter goes so far, that people who are at all strong sensitives are unable to retain a position on the left for any length of time.

Cases such as I have mentioned are innumerable in human life, and occur in thousands of connections and varieties of circumstance; they may all be accounted for and judged by the law we have just made out. And it will be recognized too what good grounds sensitives often have for their claims to consideration and forbearance.

4.

THE AURA MADE VISIBLE
BY THE AID OF
CHEMICAL SCREENS

Walter J. Kilner

*In 1908, Dr. Walter J. Kilner of London's St. Thomas'
Hospital discovered a process that enabled a person to see an
energy structure around the human body. His cautious and
detailed research focused on this method as a means of
medical diagnosis. Aware of Reichenbach's work and the
claims of sensitives, Kilner set out to systematically describe
the structure of this mysterious emanation and catalog how
it fluctuated in times of health and illness as well as how it
differed from person to person.*

In the Preface to The Human Atmosphere, *Kilner
tells how "from the first moment of seeing the human atmosphere, I determined to investigate the subject apart from all
occultism; and to remain unbiased, did not read any accounts of the aura until a large number (over sixty) of
patients had been inspected." His attempt to free himself of
the nefarious occult, however, did not spare him from the
abuse he received from the medical profession in 1912. The*
British Medical Journal *of that year compared his evidence with Macbeth's "visionary dagger." Nine years later,
this skepticism was somewhat reversed when* Medical
News *reviewed his revised edition more favorably.*

*In this selection, Kilner describes the early phase of his
research.*

* * *

Hardly one person in ten thousand is aware that he or she

is surrounded by a haze intimately connected with the body, whether asleep or awake, whether hot or cold, which, although invisible under ordinary circumstances, can be seen when conditions are favourable. This mist, the prototype of the halo or nimbus constantly depicted around the saints, has been manifested to certain individuals possessing a specially gifted sight, who have received the title of "Clairvoyants," and until quite recently, to no one else. The cloud or atmosphere, or, as it is generally termed, Aura, is the subject of this treatise, insofar as it can be perceived by the employment of screens containing a peculiar chemical substance in solution. It may as well be stated at once that we make not the slightest claim to clairvoyancy; nor are we occultists; and we especially desire to impress on our readers that our researches have been entirely physical, and can be repeated by anyone who takes sufficient interest in the subject.

As long as the faculty of perceiving the Aura is confined to a few individuals, and ordinary people have no means of corroboration or refutation, the door to imposture is open. Since this has been the case up to the present time, the subject has always been looked on askance; but there is no more charlatanism in the detection of the human Aura by the methods we employ, than in distinguishing microbes by the aid of the microscope. The main difference lies in the claim of some people that they are able to perceive the one through the possession of abnormal eyesight, while no one has had the hardihood to assert that they had the power of seeing an object one-thousandth of a millimeter in length without instrumental aid. There cannot be the smallest doubt as to the reality of the existence of an Aura enveloping human beings, and this will be in a short time an universally accepted fact, now that it can be made visible to anyone possessing normal eyesight. It would, indeed, be strange if the Aura did not vary under different circumstances, and we firmly believe that a study of its modifications will show that they will have a diagnostic value.

The discovery of a *screen* capable of making the Aura visible was by no means accidental. After reading about the actions of the "N" Rays upon phosphorescent sulphide of calcium, we were for some time experimenting on the mechanical force of certain emanations from the body, and had come to the conclusion, whether rightly or wrongly, that we had detected two forces besides heat that could act upon our needles, and that these forces were situated in the ultra-red portion of the spectrum.

There was a hitch in our experiments; and, in the early part of 1908, we thought that certain dyes might assist us. After considering the different spectra and, as far as we could, ascertaining their properties, we made trial of several, and fixed upon one which in this treatise will be called *spectauranine* as the most likely to be of use. As we were compelled to wait some time before we were able to obtain it, one night the thought flashed across us that that substance might make some portion of the above-mentioned forces visible; and, if so, we expected it would be the human Aura. This phenomenon we had heard about, but until that moment we had never had any intention of investigating it, as we believed it to be beyond our natural powers.

As soon as the chemical had been received, screens made of glass coated with collodion, and also gelatine dyed with it, were made, but were found to be entirely useless owing to decomposition taking place immediately. Afterwards a celluloid solution called *zapon* was tried. This gave a better result; but, in a few hours time, it too, lost its colour. Subsequently solutions in alcohol of different strengths in glass cells were employed. These seem on the whole to be satisfactory, but there is tendency after a time for colour changes to take place, even if kept in the dark as much as possible. As a rule only two screens are necessary: one containing a solution of spectauranine in alcohol, and a second less dilute. Others of various strengths, with and without the addition of other dyes, have been tried, but these were only for purposes of experiment under differing circumstances. For ordinary work these are unnecessary. However, another kind of screen will be found useful for differentiating the separate parts of the Aura, which will be described later on.

Directly a screen was finished, we looked at a friend through it, and instantly saw around his head and hands a faint greyish cloud, which we considered could be nothing else but the Aura. After a few minutes we were surprised to find that we could continue to see the Aura without the intervention of the screen. This power did not last long. However, it was renewed by looking at the light for a few seconds through a dark screen.

It is interesting to note that this capacity for seeing the Aura without the intervention of the screen is by no means uncommon, but generally exists only for a short while. At this period every spare moment was occupied in using the screen for this and other experiments in connection with the perception of the Aura; consequently we discovered to our cost that the spectauranine had a very deleterious effect upon our eyes, making them very painful, so much so that it was necessary to cease work for some days. On account of this, we strongly recommend all experimenters on this subject, not to be continually looking through the spectauranine screen. Apparently the action of this chemical is cumulative, so that we gradually gained the power of seeing the Aura more and more plainly without the intervention of the screen. Ultimately our eyes have become so permanently affected that under suitable conditions we are able to dispense with a screen.

The Aura can only be satisfactorily defined when certain conditions are fulfilled. The light must not be too bright. The requisite amount must be determined at each observation, and depends on whether a screen is being used or not. A rough estimate is, that the body can just be seen distinctly after the observer has become accustomed to the dullness. The light ought to be diffused, coming from one direction only, and falling on the patient equally all over. Certainly, the best arrangement is obtained when the observer is standing with his back to a darkened window while the patient faces it. An alternative method, if the room is sufficiently large and open, and the only one that can be employed at a patient's house, is to have a tent similar to the X folding portable dark-room as used for photography, except that it must be lined with black instead of the ordinary yellow material, and the front curtains must be removed. The tent is placed with its back to the window and the patient stands inside, when he will be evenly illuminated. All the windows in the room, except the one at the back of the tent, should be completely darkened, while this one must have the blind drawn more or less as required. The chief objection to this arrangement is, that the observer has to stand facing the light, which is not so comfortable for any part of the inspection, and is especially inconvenient for the observations connected with the complementary colours. Occasionally it is possible at a patient's house, with a little manoevering, to be able to place the tent with its opening facing the window. When this is done inspection is rendered much easier. It is essential to have the black background as dead black as is obtainable.

Most of our investigations have been conducted in a small room with only one window. This window is fitted at the top with an ordinary blind, and from below a blind of black serge can be raised to any height required. The serge allows a considerable amount of light to pass through, in fact too much, except on very dark days; but the amount can be regulated by pulling down the ordinary blind. This arrangement is also very convenient, as a slight gap can be left between the two blinds so as to allow much more light into the room when the patient is being observed through the dark carmine screen, and also occasionally when the complementary colours are employed.

Opposite, and about eight feet from the window is a movable pole supporting black and white curtains, either of which can be used as wanted. The white background is necessary for certain observations, which will be described further on. These are all the arrangements that are required.

There is one point that is important to bear in mind, namely, that the patient should stand about a foot in front of the background, so that shadows or marks upon it may not produce any optical illusions, and thus vitiate the observations. Trouble of this kind is not likely to occur, except when the observer is new to the work.

While the patient is assuming the proper position, the observer takes the dark screen and peers through it at the light for half a minute or longer. This will influence his eyesight for a sufficiently long time, so that it will rarely be necessary to repeat the operation. However, repetition can be made as often as desired. He now darkens the room and regulates the light; and, standing with his back to the window and opposite the patient, looks at him through a pale screen, when he ought to perceive immediately or (if not accustomed to the work) after a few seconds a faint cloud enveloping the patient, which varies in health according to individual peculiarities. If the observer has already gained the ability of perceiving the Aura without the intervention of the screen, he will usually find it to have some shade of blue. It is certainly of assistance in determining the colour of the Aura, if the patient places his hands upon his hips and at the same time extends his elbows, when, in the spaces between the trunk and the arms, the Aura emanating from the body will be reinforced by that proceeding from the arms.

When commencing a systematic inspection it will be advisable for the patient first to face the observer and the light. The Aura round the head will be best seen while he stands or sits with his hands hanging by his sides. Its breadth may roughly be determined by noticing how far it extends beyond the shoulders, and this permits the two sides to be compared, because in some cases of disease the Aura will be wider or narrower on one side than on the other. At this stage attention ought to be paid to the general shape of the Aura while the arms are hanging down, as this often differs greatly from that seen when they are uplifted. For the greater part of the inspection it will be found advantageous for the patient to stand with his hands behind his neck, so that the Aura from the axilla down the trunk, thighs, and legs may be seen uninfluenced by the Aura proceeding from the arms. This is the time to determine the shape and size of the Aura, whether it follows the contour of the body or whether it is wider by the trunk than the lower limbs; and, if so, how far it descends before it finally narrows. It is not uncommon for some abnormality of texture to be visible, but this, as a rule, can be differentiated with greater accuracy by the employment of special screens.

Occasionally the Aura can be separated by its appearance into two or, very rarely, three distinct portions, but the verification of this division will be better made at a later stage of the examination. As soon as all the information as to the Aura at the sides has been gained, the patient must be turned sideways, so that the Aura at the front and back may be similarly examined. If any suspicion should arise as to the Aura being unequally illuminated, it must be (in addition to the foregoing inspection) viewed when the back is turned to the light, and again when turned sideways in the direction opposite to the one he previously assumed. By this simple means a number of errors are eliminated. The Aura envelops the whole of the human frame, but, on account of the fineness of its texture and its transparency, it is only visible in sections; consequently when the observer wishes to examine the Aura emanating from one particular spot, he will be obliged to turn the patient to a different angle, so that a silhouette of this spot may be made on the background. Generally, if the shape of the Aura is the only thing required, it can be ascertained by the patient first standing facing the observer, and then sideways without any other movement. Considerations of the other portions of the systematic inspection must be deferred for the present.

Examination of a number of people in good health shows not merely, as might be expected, individual differences, but also the existence of a corporate dissimilarity. Males, independent of age, possess the same characteristics of the Aura, after making allowance for individual peculiarities, as no two people are alike. Quite the opposite is the case in females, because their Auras undergo a great alteration of shape at certain periods of their lives. In childhood it coincides almost exactly with that of the male. In adults it is much more developed, while in adolescence—from twelve to thirteen until eighteen to twenty years—it slowly advances from the masculine type to that of adult womanhood.

Inspection of a man discloses the Aura enveloping the head fairly equally all round, it being about two inches broader than the width of the shoulders. When he stands facing the observer, with his arms raised and his hands at the back of his neck, the Aura will appear by the side of his trunk narrower than round his head, following closely the contour of the body. Here it does not usually exceed more than four or five inches in width, or, roughly speaking, one-fifteenth of his height. As soon as he has turned sideways, it will be seen down his back about as broad as by the sides of the trunk, but barely as wide as in front. In all these cases it is similarly continued down the lower limbs, only sometimes being a little narrower. Around the arms it corresponds with that encircling the legs, but is generally broader around the hands, and very frequently it projects a long distance from the tips of the fingers.

Before a girl has arrived at the age of twelve or thirteen the description of the Aura of the males will be equally applicable to her. Nevertheless, the texture of the Aura is usually finer than that of a man, so that it occasionally becomes difficult to distinguish the edge of the haze. In like manner, but not to the same extent, the Auras of young boys may be faint. This prevents children from being good subjects for early observations. On observing the Aura of an adult woman a characteristic alteration is found. Above the shoulders round the head, down the arms and hands it is very similar to that of the males. If she faces the observer with the hands placed behind the neck, the dissimilarity is at once noticeable. The Aura is much wider by the sides of the trunk than in men, and broadens out until, at the level of the waist, it has reached its full extent. From here downwards, it gradually narrows until it reaches a point not higher than the middle of the thigh, where it finally contracts and follows the outline of the legs and feet. However, the point of final contraction may be anywhere between the place just mentioned and the ankles.

As she stands sideways, the Aura will be seen to be much wider at the back than at the front, and the broadest part is at the small of the back where it frequently bulges out. From thence it comes down from near the nates, following the contour of the legs and thighs. In front it takes the outline of the body, being a little wider at the chest and abdomen than lower down. It is not uncommon to find the haze more pronounced in front of the breasts and nipples, and this increase is evidently dependent upon the functional activity of the glands, as it is most apparent during pregnancy and lactation, but is occasionally the same just before or after menstruation. When the Aura is fully developed age does not produce any alteration, but disease may.

Amongst healthy women the Aura shows many departures from the above examples. The modifications consist in the difference of width by the side of the trunk and the distance it descends, before it has contracted to its fullest extent, and follows the contour of the body. Besides, it will be noticed that the breadth in front of the body often alters, but not nearly to the same extent. At the back, changes are more frequent and varied. These are chiefly due to differences in breadth and the position of the final contraction. With one person the outer margin of the haze is apparently quite straight from the level of the shoulders to the most prominent part of the nates, and from thence it follows the outline of the body downwards. With another person it will bulge out at the small of the back, contracting when it reaches the middle of the thigh, or it may be near the ground before it follows the figure. Occasionally the Aura proceeds downwards from over the head to the feet without coming near the body. This we consider to be the most perfect shape. Any deviations are due to undevelopment. The average width of the Aura over a woman round the waist is eight to ten inches, and on some not more than six or seven inches, but it may reach twelve or more.

When a girl approaches the age of puberty her Aura begins to show an alteration, leaving the infantile form to attain, in from four to six years, the shape assumed by an adult woman. The change does not usually commence until a short time before menstruation appears, but never before the body has begun to develop. Exceptions to this are occasionally met with. For instance, a girl fourteen years old had a marked *Transitional Aura*, but did not menstruate for six months after. The youngest child who showed any increase of Aura was thirteen and a half years old. She was a remarkably well-developed child for her age, but suffered from epileptic fits; six months previously she had an infantile Aura. Three others of fourteen, one of fifteen, four of sixteen, one of seventeen, and one of nineteen years of age, possessed Auras in a transitional state, while two others of eighteen years of age had fully formed Auras. One undersized, weakly girl, nearly seventeen years old, who had never menstruated, retained a perfectly infantile shape of Aura, which, however, was well-marked. On the other hand, a tall, well-formed young woman, twenty-five years of age, who had an undeveloped uterus, and who had only menstruated four times in her life (the last period being three years ago), is the possessor of a very distinct Aura, much larger than the average. Another woman, forty-two years of age, who had both her ovaries removed sixteen years ago, had a fairly marked Aura quite up to the average in width by the sides of the trunk, but especially broad at the back and front.

There can be no two opinions as to the enlargement of the female Aura at the period of adolescence, but it remains to be proved whether this is entirely due to the functional maturity of the sexual organs, or whether the other changes which have taken place in the system contribute to its development. But this much can be confidently stated, as will appear later on, that menstruation has a subtle effect on the Aura, while the changes in shape in early pregnancy are not very pronounced. During a later period a great extension in front of the breast and the lower part of the abdomen may appear, but this is only temporary and local.

For the sake of simplicity, and to avoid unnecessary repetition in the above description, the Aura has been treated as if it were a simple phenomenon, while in reality it is composite.

First, there is a narrow transparent portion appearing as a dark space, which is very often obliterated by the second portion of the Aura. When visible it looks like a dark band, not exceeding a quarter of an inch, surrounding and adjacent to the body, without any alteration in size at any part. This will be called the *Etheric Double*.

The second constituent is the *Inner Aura*. It is the densest portion and varies comparatively little, or even not at all, in width, either at the back, front, or sides, and both in the male and the female follows the contour of the body. It arises just outside the Etheric Double, but very frequently it looks as if it touched the body itself.

The third portion, or the *Outer Aura*, commences at the outer edge of the Inner Aura, and is very variable in size. It is the extreme outer margin of this that has been taken for depicting the outline of the Aura hitherto. When the whole Aura is observed through a light spectauranine screen, or a pale-blue one, all the portions appear blended together, but the part nearest the body is the most dense. If, however, a carmine screen be employed, each of the factors will be distinguished; or, should this screen be a fairly dark one, the Outer Aura will be eliminated altogether.

5

THE APPEARANCE OF
THE NORMAL AURA

Oscar Bagnall

Cambridge biologist Oscar Bagnall's independent research improved the work of Walter J. Kilner. In The Origins and Properties of the Human Aura *published in 1937, Bagnall comments that he could not verify some of Kilner's observations with the dicyanin screens and speculates that Kilner probably had some clairvoyant ability.*

Bagnall proposes that the aura is primarily seen by the rods, the sensory neurons in the retina that function exclusively at night or in dim light; the cones are for color and clear vision. He suggests that Kilner may have been aware of this because he advised one never to strain the eyes by staring hard at the outline of a body. According to Bagnall, "Since the rods lie to the side of the center part of the retina, which is lined solely by cones and which receives the direct image of the object being viewed, it would . . . clearly be an advantage to look at the object, if not out of the corner of one's eye, at least not by peering hard and directly at it." Because the rods function more slowly than the cones, this could explain Kilner's observation that the aura usually did not appear all at once.

Bagnall's work, generally disregarded before World War II, now not only provides us with concise methods of viewing the aura, but as this selection reveals, offers intriguing ideas about its gradual development.

* * *

In the neighborhood of the skin and extending from it

for some three inches, there is a brighter aura which appears to be more solid than that beyond it. It seems to be made up of lines very close together, running directly away from the body. It hugs the body fairly closely—I mean by this that it is of much the same shape as the body, only extended a few inches beyond it on either side. I am presuming that the subject being inspected is standing facing the observer.

This *inside aura* varies in brightness with the health of its owner. Extending some six to eight inches beyond this is an *outer haze*, which gradually fades away at its distal margin, but which is more or less oval in shape. It has been claimed that the color of this will vary. Some say that the aura can be red, gold, brown, or all sorts of colors, depending upon the character of the person emitting it. I am not going to contradict this, of course. Personally, I have not seen it. The aura, this outer haze, has always been misty, pale blue to pale gray, when I have seen it. The better the intellect of the subject, the bluer the haze. The word "intellect" is, perhaps, vague. I have seen a blue haze emanating from those who may be described as being mentally alert or as having good intellectual development.

The inside aura looks much the same in all of us—men, women, and children. Not so the outer haze. Up to the age of puberty, it protrudes only some four inches beyond the brighter inside aura. From about the age of fourteen to eighteen, a woman's aura gradually widens until it attains about eight inches (nearly a foot in all), becoming oval, the widest part being about the waistline.

This widening does not take place in the aura of man, and for this reason women prove the more satisfactory subjects.

The inside part of the aura has always been distinctly brighter than the haze beyond it; and there is, to me, a fairly clear boundary between them. One must not conclude, though, as soon as the eyes have been temporarily sensitized by the screen for the first time, that each of one's fellow beings is thereafter going to appear surrounded by a dazzling halo which in turn will be bathed in

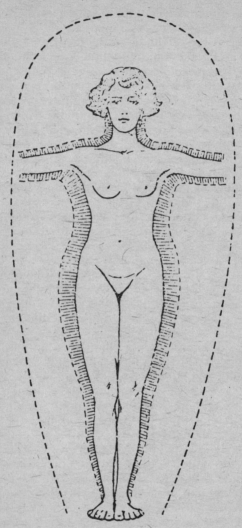

Woman, normal aura.

a kind of sunset effect. This quite decidedly does not happen.

Having gazed at the sky (not directly at the sun) through a dark dicyanin screen for a minute or two, next cast the eyes around, still keeping the screen in place. If you are in a garden or in a country district, the foliage appears a plum color and soon seems to become hazy. Care should be taken before affixing the screen to see that the glasses are dry and that all moisture is removed from the face near the eyes. The mistiness which would thus be caused is not entirely unlike the haze when it first begins to appear.

Next examine the hands. It seems as if steam is rising from them. Place the tips of the fingers of one hand against the tips of the corresponding ones of the other. Then draw them slowly apart. The lines should be observed running from finger to finger.

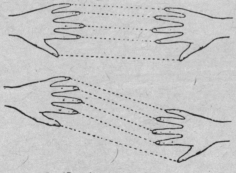

Rays between the fingers.

It may occur to some of my readers that this is simply an optical illusion, the lines appearing to remain in the path traveled by the fingers. This suspicion can easily be set at rest. If the hands are drawn apart aslant—for example, by pushing the left hand away and drawing the right toward the body, as shown in the diagram, it will be found that the connecting lines run diagonally also.

Again, one cannot make these lines curve, they are always straight lines.

Rays of light travel in straight lines. Ultraviolet rays must do so, too.

Notice also that the haze extends farther around the tips of the fingers than around their shanks.

It is unlikely that more than this will be seen at the first attempt, for the action of the dye is cumulative. Later on, it will be found that, having sensitized the eyes for some two or three minutes as described, one can dispense with the screen, or replace it with a much weaker one, and that the aura will remain visible for sometime afterward, the length of time depending on the accumulation acquired, and to some extent upon the eyes. Some people see the aura much more clearly as well as more quickly than others do. . . . Variations in weather conditions will make some difference—to the material part of the aura as well as to the absorption of its ultraviolet rays. Changes of temperature, treated purely as such, have no influence so far as I have been able to discover.

The brighter inside aura appears, as I have said, to follow the outline of the body, extending from it some three inches. It seems to be made up of a number of small rays (as undoubtedly it is) running parallel to one another and at right angles to the body.

Sometimes longer, and still brighter, pencils of rays extend from the proximal edge of this aura beyond it so as to encroach upon, or possibly to extend beyond, the outer haze. These rays, of course, travel in straight lines, though not necessarily parallel to those of the aura.

They are, in all probability, of the same origin as the aura, and have been seen to run toward some prominent object near the body—even an inanimate object, such as the pole of a bar magnet.

These rays may be observed stretching from one part (probably from a projection) of the body to another. For example, when the hands are raised above the head, rays may be seen to extend beyond the inside aura both from the head and from the arm and to link together in the space between so as to make a continuous pencil of rays from head to arm. Because the rays from the head are somewhat brighter than those from the arms, the pencils have the appearance of running from head to arms. The whole phenomenon is possibly a kind of auric attraction in such a case.

Occasionally *other* bundles of rays have been noticed extending through the outer haze and out beyond, heading nowhere in particular. These rays, too, are brighter than the rest of the aura. Imagine oneself looking down from a cliff onto a sea front along which are a row of bright lamps throwing a gleam out into the water. The sea front corresponds to the skin, the gleam of the lamps to the inside aura. A searchlight throwing its beam across the sea, not necessarily at right angles to the sea front, possibly diagonally, would well represent this stronger bundle of rays.

These rays must either be given out by some part of the body, differing from the rest of the auric emission for some specific reason, or drawn away from it by some external attracting force. I at first inclined to the latter view. If this were the case, it would mean that the inside aura was sufficiently elastic to allow these flagellalike rays to be drawn out to some three times their natural visible length. The obvious drawback to this view is that it does not satisfactorily account for the additional brightness of such rays when compared with the rest of the aura. With the improved screen I am using today, I have been able to see a little farther into the ultraviolet region in which it appears that the wavelength of these rays lies. I am convinced now that they are of outer haze origin, since I have been unable to show that they possess mass. . . .

In order that I might the more easily examine one of the constituent parts of the aura, it has been necessary to dim the other in an attempt to exclude its influence.

If the aura is examined through a *red* screen, the outer haze becomes less obvious, and so a better estimate can be formed as to the exact distal margin of the inside aura.

This experiment is not possible, of course, until one's

eyes have reached that stage of accumulation where the aura can be seen after the removal of the dicyanin screen.

I have found, too, that a *blue* screen tends:

1. To make the distal margin of the outer haze much more obvious.
2. To make the inside aura look brighter, though less sharply defined.

I find that this screen is tending not so much to obliterate the inside aura as to intensify the outer haze which I believe to lie beneath it or, rather, to be intermingling with it.

The outer haze, I consider, originates partly from the skin. Thus it will run through the inside aura beyond which it extends.

Perhaps I ought to say that this opinion is entirely contrary to that of others, and so to the generally accepted one, so far as there are any accepted opinions in what is, comparatively speaking, an uncharted sea of scientific research.

I have noticed a blank space, a void, between the skin and the inside aura. It has the appearance of a dark band and is not more than an eighth of an inch wide.

Dr. Kilner claims that this void is always present. He called it the "Etheric Double," and treated it as a possible third constituent part of the whole aura. He even went so far as to say that it appeared to him to be very slightly pink-tinted.

I feel, however, that few of us can hope to see what Kilner saw, for he was undoubtedly singularly gifted in this respect—clairvoyant. I have tested most of his claims and I can vouch for the majority of them from my personal experience. Others I do not for one moment presume to doubt, though I have never been able to confirm them, because my eyes can see no farther beyond the violet than most other people's, except, of course, artificially.

I certainly think that what I have seen others can see

too, provided that they have average sight. I am convinced that clairvoyance, like hands in a horseman or wrists in a batsman, is a gift of the gods, and cannot be acquired by any marked degree. Dicyanin does give one a good lift along the road into the ultraviolet, however. I tell you everything I can, like the White Knight—and really there is little enough to relate, for I am determined to set down only what I have seen.

Let us now turn our attention to the outer haze —mystical, a thing of moods, changeable as Proteus, and teeming with possibilities. *Praeter opiniones* I cannot think of this haze as beginning where the inside aura leaves off. It, too, is clearly emitted from some source within the body.

If the outer haze be examined through a blue screen so as to intensify it, and thus obscure the inside aura by comparison (it is, as a general rule, difficult to dim this part of the aura without obliterating the outer haze as well), it will be noticed that the inside aura seems less striated, taking on more of the misty appearance of the outer haze. It will be remembered that the inside aura appears as horizontal rays running outward from and at right angles to the skin, while the outer haze is misty rather than striped. Clearly, then, since the outer haze has been intensified and the usually brighter inside aura by comparison dimmed, it is fair to infer that one is viewing the outer haze running through the inside aura, and to presume that it, too, emanates from somewhere under the skin. The blue screen I have used for this viewing is one containing a solution of blue (not violet) pinacyanol, which acts as a sensitizer at the same time.

The distal margin is nothing hard and fast, but the haze can certainly be considered as having a definite shape. In children of either sex and also in men, the haze is comparatively narrow and possibly brighter than it is in the case of women; for it seems to be closer knit, compressed, following more or less the shape of the body only to a lesser degree than does the inside aura. Males and children, therefore, make relatively uninteresting subjects for the examination of this haze, and my remarks will apply in particular to the much wider haze that can be seen surrounding a woman. The shape is roughly oval, being widest at the waistline and tapering gradually toward the ankles. The haze is less compact than it is in the case of a man, the distal edge is less clearly defined —uncertain, a thing unleashed, groping away into space. Indefinite, it is true, but tremendously interesting.

May I emphasize that I have found nothing whatever to suggest that *this haze* could possibly represent an electric field around the body. It does not seem to be material, that is, it has no appreciable mass. There is little doubt in my mind that it consists of rays, the wavelength of which is not in normal conditions visible to the human eye.

Just as a horse's coat or a dog's nose gives an indication of its physical condition, so the inside aura changes, being brighter and sharper in outline when a person is in robust health. In like manner the outer haze may be said to register mental development. As mentioned before, the only color I have ever seen imparted to the haze, disregarding pathological cases, has varied from pale blue to pale gray. The bluer and the finer the haze, the better the intellect—that is the general rule. If a body emits a haze that is gray and dull, it usually houses wits that are dull also. An important qualification should be added here, that the color of the haze is also affected by the pigmentation of the skin, and dark-skinned races tend to have grayer hazes.

Gray hazes vary from blue-gray to the drab gray (almost brown-tinted gray) of the Negro.

The haze surrounding a very young baby is rather greenish, with little differentiation between the inside and the outer parts of the aura.

It is difficult to determine the exact point in life when one acquires an aura—it is certainly considerably earlier than birth. Newly born babies always have an aura, though it is not always obvious without a suitable background. I have suggested that the widening of the aura of a pregnant woman, particularly as the time of birth approaches, may be because her own aura is augmented by that of the unborn baby. Often, too, her aura is brighter as well as wider over the abdominal region. The law rules that life begins at birth. Biology has proved that *conception* marks our beginning; for the zygote nucleus in the original cell undoubtedly lives and is created sexually by two individuals, as can be demonstrated by following the division of the micronucleus in an animal as elementary as the unicellular paramoecium.

Women who are mothers speak of their babies having come to life (or quickened) at a particular time during pregnancy, usually about three or four months after conception. The wider aura has been noticed as being permanently present as early as that. The widening seen at the beginning of pregnancy is not permanent and cannot be attributed to the formation of the aura of the embryo, since it occurs also with the onset of menstruation. . . .

I feel that the aura is emitted at this point (five or six months before birth), though the question of the embryo aura necessarily entails more guesswork than scientific argument can safely carry. If it is emitted then, why should it not be emitted earlier in life, even from the moment of conception? My impression is that all living things emit an aura, though just where in the solar spectrum the wavelengths of the component rays lie in the various creatures—and so the possibility of their becoming visible to the human eye—it has as yet been impossible to find out. I have been concentrating my research only upon rendering visible auric rays whose wavelength is just a little shorter than that of the violet end of the visible spectrum. The aura emitted by the human embryo in the early days after conception, if such an aura be emitted, would surely be made up of ultraviolet rays—I do not see that any form of metamorphosis can alter the wavelength—but an aura so feeble as this necessarily must be would not be made visible by screens in their present state of comparative imperfection.

The beginning thus corresponds more or less to the beginning of life, and the intensity increases gradually as the embryo gains in size and strength. The aura persists as long as life lasts, and seems to cease to be emitted the moment death has taken place.

While there is an aura, there is life—and, presumably, as soon as there is life, an aura will be emitted.

6.

THE ENERGY FIELD

John C. Pierrakos

John C. Pierrakos is a psychiatrist and scientist who has studied the energy fields of human beings, animals, plants and crystals for twenty years. He is director of the Institute for Bioenergetic Analysis in New York and a co-director of The Energy Research Group. In this selection he offers his observations of the aura, stressing its unique rhythmic, vibrational, and color qualities in each individual. He has attempted to use these observations diagnostically in his psychiatric practice.

* * *

In nature there are several groups of unicellar organisms; such as bacteria and fungi, and also multicellular structures; such flagellates, sponges, fish and fireflies that are able to emit light and "luminate" as the result of their inner movements and biological processes. In higher organisms, it is known that vital processes such as mitosis of cells, oxidation, and other metabolic processes are accompanied by luminescence. Living organisms are able to emit light through the entire surface of their bodies; they have not lost their ability to luminate. This phenomena constitutes the energy field, or Aura, which is, in effect, a reflection of the energies of life processes. (Aura comes from the Greek *avra*, which means breeze.) The aura, or energy field, is a light cast of the body energies. Energy comes from the word *energeia*, which means to produce movement or work. A more functional definition is that "Energy is the living force emanated by consciousness." Consciousness was previously related to perceiving oneself through the inner pulsatory movements expressed, on the surface, as the energy field.

The field phenomena are related to the energy metabolism of the body, its production of heat, emotional excitement, rate and quality of breathing, activity, and rest. They are also affected by atmospheric conditions, relative humidity, polarity of charges in the air, and many other unknown factors.

If one could see this luminous phenomenon around the body, which exists also in the space between people, one would perceive that human beings swim in a sea of fluid, tinged rhythmically with brilliant colors which constantly change hues, shimmer, and vibrate. For being alive is to be colorful and vibrant.

The field phenomena belong, in addition, to another dimension. They are energetic phenomena that transcend the physical realities of matter and, even though they are tied up with the structure and matter of the body, they have their own laws of pulsatory movement and vibration not yet understood.

To come to a more practical definition of this phenomenon, as in my observations, I can say the following:

When a person stands against a homogeneous background, either very light (sky blue) or very dark (midnight blue), and with certain arrangements so that there is a softness and uniformity in the light, one can clearly see, with the air of colored filters (cobalt blue) or with the unaided eye, a most thrilling phenomenon. From the periphery of the body arises a cloudlike, blue-gray envelope which extends for 2 to 4 feet where it loses its distinctness and merges with the surrounding atmosphere. This envelope is brilliant and illuminates the periphery of the body in the same way as the rays of the rising sun light up the fringes of dark mountains. It swells slowly, for 1 to 2 seconds, away from the body until it forms a nearly perfect oval shape with fringed edges. It remains in full development for approximately 1/4 of a second and then, abruptly, it disappears completely. It takes about 1/5 to 1/8 of a second to vanish. Then there is a pause of 1 to 3 seconds until it reappears again to repeat the process. This process is repeated 15 to 25 times a minute in the average resting person.

The envelope is roughly divided into three layers. First there is an inner dark blue-black layer of approximately 1/5 to 1/8 of an inch. Second, there is the middle blue-gray layer of about 3 to 4 inches, and the third is an outer sky-blue layer of about 6 to 8 inches. (See Figures A and B).

Attempting to describe the exact consistency and features of these three layers is extremely difficult. The first, or inner layer, can be seen only when the observer is close to the subject, about 2 or 3 feet away. It is completely transparent and looks like an empty, dark space. It has a crystallinelike quality and its true color is on the borderline of ultraviolet and violet in the spectrum. It can be seen best against a dull, black background and appears to reproduce the form of the body in space.

The second, or intermediate layer, is a complex one to describe as it is made up of a multiple of shapes and forms. It starts at the outer boundary of the inner layer and is clearly defined. Its overall color is blue-gray and it is brilliant, especially around the head: "the halo of saints." It has, primarily, 3 patterns of movements. First, there is a wavelike form which homogeneously fills the whole layer to its extremes; like ink on blotting paper. Second, there is a corpuscular movement similar to those seen under a microscope in smoke particles: the so-called brownian movement. Third, there is a linear movement in the form of white or yellow rays that commence at the inner border of the intermediate layer, travel its whole width and extend several feet away from the body into space, almost reaching the walls of the room. In spite of this outer movement, the intermediate layer is dominated in the trunk and extremities by a wavelike movement that moves distinctly along the surface of the body. Its overall appearance is that of a blue, shimmering

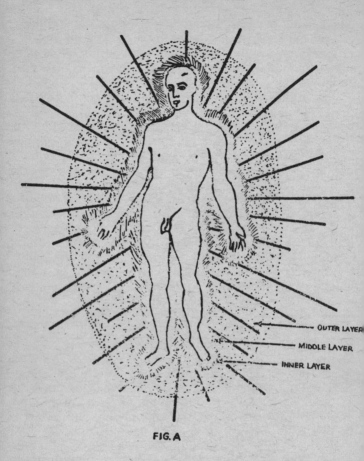

OUTER LAYER
MIDDLE LAYER
INNER LAYER

FIG. A

liquid, extremely rarified, but brilliant. The impression gained is that of a stream of fireflies extinguishing their glow at rapid intervals and progressing simultaneously in the same direction. The raylike movement is dominant and very brilliant around the head where it forms a fringelike effect. The pattern and outline changes with every new pulsation of the organism in the same manner as when the aurora borealis fires towards the sky, in rapid succession, brilliant streamers. Usually, the raylike movement is perpendicular to the surface of the body.

The third, or outer layer, is 6 to 8 inches wide but, in an open space, it expands several dozen feet away. And,

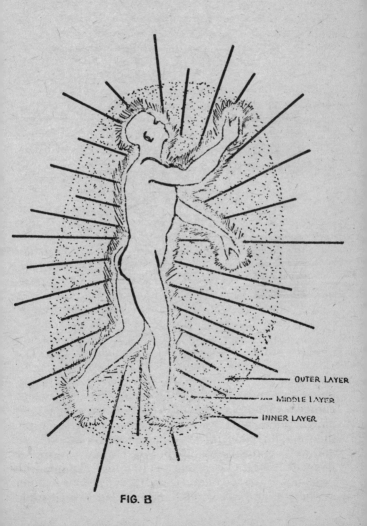

OUTER LAYER

MIDDLE LAYER

INNER LAYER

FIG. B

near the shore it has been seen to extend as far as 100 feet from the person emanating such energies. It has an indefinite inner body commencing at the outer boundaries of the middle layer. It is a very thin, practically transparent, and has a delicate sky-blue color. It is also transversed by the vertical rays which commence in the middle layer. The predominant movement of this layer is spiral or vortical. It appears as though the particulate of brownianlike movement of the second layer, finding greater space, expands in all directions in the same way as compressed gas molecules are allowed to expand by increasing the volume of the container. The outer boundaries of the third layer become so diffused that its margins are lost in the surrounding air. Its general direction of movement is perpendicular to the surface of the organism.

The direction of movement of the 3 layers, which as far as I can see move simultaneously, is somewhat complicated. Facing the subject we can clearly perceive the energy field on the sides of the trunk, head, arms, and legs. We observe then that the field moves from the ground up on the inner side of the legs and thighs, up the trunk and the outer side of the hands, forearms, and arms; and the two main streams meet and travel upwards towards the neck and over the head. This is phase one of the movement. At the same time there is a movement on the inside of the trunk towards the ground. This is phase two. It is interesting to note that there is an alternating upward and downward movement in each half of the body; each half has a simultaneous upward and downward flow. The streams join at the root of the neck and travel to the opposite half of the head. The alteration in the direction of movement of the field is represented in the alternate shifting in the two halves of the body, as when walking or running, and changing one's place on the surface of the earth. Both these alternate phases of the field fuse in the middle line of the body longitudinally. Thus, upon observing the field while the subject stands in profile, we see that the field pulsates from the mid-section, located in the area of the vital organs, towards the head and feet simultaneously in both the front and the back sides of the body. The assumption is made here that there must be a multitude of movements of the field inside the body, engulfing the body as well as the vital organs, such as the heart, lungs, liver, and the intestines, in a spiral motion. This is supported by the shape of these organs and their spontaneous twisting and turning movements.

However, if we compare the human organism with a flexible cylinder, we see that there can be basically two kinds of movements; one along its longitudinal axis, another along its diameter. All other movements are resulting forces of these two main directions. The longitudinal movement, if applied against the supporting base of the cylinder, can move the cylinder from one place on the surface of the earth to another. This is done, in the human body, in walking and moving. The movement along its diameter can be towards the center or away from it. And, if they are flexible, it can inflate or deflate the walls of the cylinder. This type of movement has to do with the phases of expansion and contraction of the body. This primordial movement is of utmost importance in primitive organisms such as the amoeba. In man, both movements are an expression of each other. The longitudinal movement keeps the body erect, the transverse makes the organism expand and contract. . . .

The following is an explanation, from my observations, of what makes up the movement of the energy field:

There is a basic longitudinal movement in the core of the human cylinder emanating from the vital organs as the field moves upwards towards the head or downwards towards the feet. It, also, rapidly permeates, in a radial fashion, all the tissues irrespective of anatomical configuration, and reaches towards the periphery of the body. It, then, passes the skin and excites the surrounding atmosphere, creating the visual perception of the phenomenon of the energy field with its three layers.

What we see, actually, are the changes in the surrounding atmosphere in the same way that we observe steam rising above boiling water. The steam molecules are of the same nature as the boiling water; only of different status, which is gaseous. In the same manner, the energy field seen in the envelope surrounding the human organism is a modified form of the energy flowing inside the body. By studying its characteristics, we can find out its true movement, composition, and consistency and the changes that occur in pathological conditions or in the simple processes of life with its variations. The energy field is actually a reflection of the multitude of energies moving and expanding in all directions within the living body.

7.

DEVELOPING AURIC SIGHT

S. G. J. Ouseley

Try the following simple tests to see the aura. Note well the final paragraph of this extract from a pamphlet first published in 1949.

* * *

A Preliminary Test

A simple test by which the experimenter may discover whether he or she is sensitive to auric radiations may be made as follows:—

When you go to bed at night take an ordinary iron magnet with you. Having put the light out and made the room as pitch-dark as possible get into bed and be relaxed for a minute or two. It is important to make your mind as passive as possible. Then holding the magnet under the bedclothes gaze steadily upon it. You must of course lift the clothes but the magnet itself should be quite invisible to you. You can tell where it is by touch. After a few moments you should be able to see a faint pale light hovering round the poles of the magnet. The light will vary in intensity according to the degree of auric clairvoyance you possess. You may see just a misty patch of light or clearly defined rays. If either phenomenon occurs it shows that you possess actual power for seeing the aura.

If you fail to see any light the first or second time don't give up. You should allow a week or a fortnight to test yourself.

This is a simple, elementary test. If you wish to develop

auric sight a step further then you can experiment by concentrating your sensing faculty on another person. Choose someone with whom you are in harmony. A dark curtain or some dark unpolished material should be hung up in a quiet room on the wall opposite the window. The subject stands or sits about twelve or eighteen inches away from the dark curtain with what little light there is falling evenly on him.

With some observers, it is preferable to have the subject as far as possible unclothed, but it is not essential.

If the experiment is being made in the daytime, you should stand at the window and gaze at the sky—not the sun—for half a minute; if after dark, it will be sufficient to gaze at the electric light for the same length of time. You should then close your eyes, sit down, relax, and endeavour to become as passive as possible. Concentrate mentally on the idea of the aura. Be careful to avoid making an effort of will. Gaze calmly at the subject and note the formation of any mist, lights, or rays in any region of his or her body. Do not be easily discouraged if nothing is seen. Patient and regular practice is as necessary in developing auric sight as any other form of psychic development. Colours in the aura are not always seen objectively, but they may be "felt" or sensed.

The head seems the main field for the manifestation of the aura. It has been found that those who are above the average in mental power and alertness have a much broader and clearly defined auric base round the head than those with weak intellects. It is interesting to note that the male and female auras have different characteristics. As a rule the female aura appears larger and better developed. The rays seem capable of being influenced by the will of the person possessing them and it will be found that some women are able to project them from any part of the body, or even to change their colour.

Experiment with the Hands

The subject is asked to place the fingertips of both

hands together for upwards of a minute and then slowly draw them apart. Auric radiations can be seen issuing from the tips of the fingers and uniting each hand. A small group of people can participate in this experiment. The best method is to lay an unglazed black cloth on the table. Each experimenter must relax and try mentally to visualize the aura. It will be found that some form of soft music or singing helps in bringing about the desired atmosphere. The hands rest upon the table palms downwards. When the fingers are pointed towards an experimenter opposite the etheric rays will be seen to reach across and unite.

Each pair of sitters will be seen united in the same way. Around many hands a dark line may be seen intervening between the fingers and the aura surrounding them. The outer edge of the aura emits rays of varying colour and intensity. The hands of the more vital and sensitive people appear to radiate sunlight whilst others remain normal. The latter is not likely to develop but an improvement may occur by changing the sitter next to him. When auras cannot be made to blend, phenomena will not occur.

If there are several sensitives among the experimenters the aura from all hands blends in the centre like a luminous cloud composed of rapidly moving auric particles.

Colour Exercise

To develop colour awareness in the seeing of auras, it is a beneficial exercise to place some slips of brightly coloured paper in different envelopes. Sit in an easy chair or recline on a couch or bed in a comfortable position. Devote a few minutes to deep breathing which will bring about a state of relaxation.

Breathe deeply and slowly until no more air can be inhaled. Then hold the breath and bear the full lung pressure down on the pit of the stomach for a few seconds after which exhale gradually until the lungs are entirely emptied of air. This breathing must be done under conscious control of the mind. During the exercise visualize the seven Major Colour Rays.

Make a mental picture of a globe of light which is constantly changing colour. First red, then orange, yellow, green, blue, indigo, and violet. After a few minutes of colour concentration hold one of the envelopes in your hand or against the middle of your forehead and try to visualize the colour within.

Sometimes the auric emanations will be seen to settle on the hands of one or other of the sitters—usually the most sensitive person present.

It is usual to make the first half hour of experiments in full light. In the second half hour, when concentration and practice have induced passivity, the experiments may be made in semi-darkness.

With most people auric vision does not come in a few days or even months. It is a lifetime study and one's life and habits must be on a high plane to get good results. The finer forces are not discernible to the eyes of the gross materialist or the seeker after wonders and sensations. It is not to be considered that "having eyes they see not." The study and practice of seeing the aura is not to be lightly entered upon. It is a serious and priceless power and should be utilized for the upliftment and betterment of humanity.

Part Two

Man's Inner Structure: the Psychic Experience

8.

AURAS

Edgar Cayce

The late American clairvoyant Edgar Cayce produced a body of about fourteen million words while in a trancelike sleep. This series of "readings" covered an enormous range of questions put to him, many of which concerned individual health problems.

This account of the aura, emphasizing the implications of what it means to see it, comes from a booklet Cayce worked on with Thomas Sugrue, his close friend and biographer, shortly before his death on January 3, 1945.

* * *

Ever since I can remember I have seen colors in connection with people. I do not remember a time when the human beings I encountered did not register on my retina with blues and greens and reds gently pouring from their heads and shoulders. It was a long time before I realized that other people did not see these colors; it was a long time before I heard the word aura, and learned to apply it to this phenomenon which to me was commonplace. I do not ever think of people except in connection with their auras; I see them change in my friends and loved ones as time goes by—sickness, dejection, love, fulfillment—these are all reflected in the aura, and for me the aura is the weather vane of the soul. It shows

67

which way the winds of destiny are blowing.

Many people are able to see auras; many have had experiences similar to mine—not knowing for many years that it was something unique. One of my friends, a lady, who is a member of the association told me this:

All during my childhood I saw colors in connection with people, but did not realize that it was uncommon. One day the appearance of a woman in our neighborhood struck me as odd, though I could not for the moment see anything strange about her. When I got home it suddenly struck me that she had no colors about her. Within a few weeks this woman died. That was my first experience with what I have learned to look upon as a natural action of nature.

Apparently the aura reflects the vibrations of the soul. When a person is marked for death the soul begins to withdraw and the aura naturally fades. At the end there is only a slim connection and the break is easy. I have heard that when people died suddenly, in accidents, the passing was very difficult because the way had not been prepared.

A person's aura tells a great deal about him, and when I understood that few people saw it and that it had a spiritual significance, I began to study the colors with an idea of discovering their meaning. Over a period of years I have built up a system which from time to time I have checked with other persons who see auras. It is interesting to note that in almost all interpretation these other people and I agree. We only differ with regard to the colors which are in our own auras. This is curious, for it shows how universal are nature's laws. We know that opposites attract and likes repel. Well, I have a lot of blue in my aura and my interpretation of this color does not always jibe with that of a person whose aura does not contain it and who therefore interprets it objectively. One lady I know has a great deal of green in her aura, and she is inclined to dislike green in the aura of others, and place a disagreeable interpretation on it, whereas it is the color of healing and a fine one to have.

Occasionally I have found in books devoted to occult sciences, definitions of colors, and these are generally in accord with what I have found by experience to be true. The reading of any particular aura, however, is a skill that is gained over a long period of time by constant observation and endless trial and error. The intermingling of the colors, their relationship one to another, and the dominance of one over the other, are matters which must be considered before rendering a judgment. I am generally better able to "read" persons I know than strangers, although certain general characteristics of the strangers, strike me immediately. But to be helpful I find it best to know the individual. Then I can tell him when I see the twinkling lights of success and achievement, or warn him when melancholy or illness threaten. Of course I do not do this professionally. I would not think of such a thing. But I believe it is an ability which all people will someday possess, and therefore I want to do what I can to get folks used to the idea of auras, so they will think in terms of auras, so they will begin to attempt to see themselves.

I have been told that with proper equipment it is possible for almost anyone to see an aura. Equipment has been built for this purpose, and I once met a professor who said that he not only had seen auras but in his laboratory had measured and weighed them.

Where do the colors come from, and what makes them shift and change? Well, color seems to be a characteristic of the vibration of matter, and our souls seem to reflect it in this three-dimensional world through atomic patterns. We are patterns, and we project colors, which are there for those who can see them.

In his remarkable book, *Pain, Sex, and Time*, Gerald Heard, speaking of the evidence for the evolution of consciousness, points out that our ability to see colors is expanding. The easiest color to see, as you know, is red. At that end of the spectrum the waves of light are long. At the other end, where blue runs into indigo and violet, the waves are short. According to Heard, who is a reliable scholar, our ability to see blue is very recent. Natives who live on the Blue Nile in Africa do not know it by that name. Their title for it, when translated, means brown. Homer, all through the *Iliad* and *Odyssey*, describes the Mediterranean as the "wine-dark sea." Mr. Heard says that apparently Homer caught "the slight tinge of red in the purple of the Mediterranean," but did not see its predominant blue. Aristotle, moreover, said that the rainbow had only three colors: red, yellow, and green. We all know that perspective in painting is recent, and it is apparently undeveloped in many primitive people to this day, for travelers in the remote Pacific Islands have found that natives looking at motion pictures are unable to perceive anything but a flat surface—their eyes cannot give three-dimensionality to the pictures.

So it would seem that our eyes gradually are gaining in power. I have heard many people comment on the prevalence of spectacles among our civilized people. They have seemed to consider this a bad thing. Could it be that it is a result of constant straining on the part of our eyes to see more and to bring us to the next step of evolution? I think this is true and will be recognized in the future. The Japanese, for instance, are just emerging from a medieval civilization, and in attempting to see the things we already perceive they have strained their eyes so that most every one of them wears glasses.

What will it mean to us if we make this next evolutionary step? Well, it will mean that we can see auras. What will this mean? I am going to answer that by telling two experiences of a friend of mine who is able to see auras.

This person, a woman, told me this:

Whenever a person, whether it be a stranger, an intimate friend, or a member of my family, decides to tell me an untruth, or to evade a direct and frank answer to a question of mine, I see a streak of lemony green shoot through his aura, horizontally, just over his head. I call it gaslight green, and I have never known it to fail as an indication of evasion or falsification. I was a school teacher for many years, and my students marveled at my ability to catch them in any detour from the truth.

Imagine what that will mean—everyone able to see when you plan to tell them a lie, even a little white one. We will all have to be frank, for there will no longer be such a thing as deceit!

Now let me tell you the other incident.

One day in a large city I entered a department store to do some shopping. I was on the sixth floor and rang for the elevator. While I was waiting for it I noticed some bright red sweaters, and thought I would like to look at them. However, I had signaled for the elevator, and when it came I stepped forward to enter it. It was almost filled with people, but suddenly I was repelled. The interior of the car, although well-lighted, seemed dark to me. Something was wrong. Before I could analyze my action I said, "Go ahead," to the operator, and stepped back. I went over to look at the sweaters, and then I realized what had made me uneasy. The people in the elevator had no auras. While I was examining the sweaters, which had attracted me by their bright red hues—the color of vigor and energy—the elevator cable snapped, the car fell to the basement, and all the occupants were killed.

You see what the knack of seeing auras will mean when it becomes a common ability. Danger, catastrophe, accidents, death, will not come unannounced. We will see them on their way as did the prophets of old; and as the prophets of old we will recognize and welcome our own death, understanding its true significance.

It is difficult to project ourselves into such a world, a

world where people will see each other's faults and virtues, their weaknesses and strength, their sickness, their misfortunes, their coming success. We will see ourselves as others see us and we will be an entirely different type of person, for how many of our vices will persist when all of them are known to everyone?

One more comment on the possibilities of the future; then we will return to the more mundane present. Another person who sees auras once told me this:

> If I am talking to a person and he makes a statement of opinion which reflects a prejudice gained in one of his former lives, I see as he speaks a figure in his aura, which is a reflection of the personality he was in that time—I see, that is, the body of a Greek, or an Egyptian, or whatever he happened to be. As soon as we pass on to another subject and the opinion gained in that incarnation passes, the figure disappears. Later he will express another view. Perhaps he will say, "I have always loved Italy and wanted to go there," and as he speaks I will see the figure of a Renaissance man or an old Roman. During the course of an afternoon's conversation I may see six or eight of these figures.

Well, what is that but a Life Reading, except for the interpretations and judgments? It sounded so strange when I heard it that I was inclined to be skeptical, until one evening at dusk when, sitting on the porch of a friend's house, I saw the thing myself. My friend was speaking earnestly to a group of people, and he made some interpretation of English history. In his aura I saw the figure of a young monk, and I recalled that in his Life Reading this friend had been identified as a monk in England.

"But what do auras mean to the majority of people, who cannot see them?" you ask. Well, the majority of people do see them, I believe, but do not realize it. I believe anyone can figure out what another person's aura is in a general way, if he will take note of the colors which a person habitually uses in the matter of clothing and decoration. How many times have you said of a woman, "Why does she wear that color? It does not suit her at all." How many times have you said, "How beautiful she looks in that dress. The color is just right for her. She was made to wear it." In both cases you have been reading an aura. The first woman was wearing a color which clashed with her aura. The second woman was wearing a color which harmonized with her aura. All of you know what colors are helpful to your friends, and bring out the best in them. They are the colors that beat with the same vibrations as the aura, and thus strengthen and heighten it. By watching closely you can even discover changes in your friends as they are reflected in a shift in the color predominating in their wardrobe.

Let me give you an example, one that has to do with health as it is indicated in the aura. I knew a man who from boyhood wore nothing but blue—frequently I have seen him with a blue suit, blue shirt, blue tie, and even blue socks. One day he went into a store to buy some ties. He was surprised to find that he had selected several which were maroon in color. He was even more surprised when as time went on, he began to choose shirts with garnet stripes and ties and pocket handkerchief sets in various shades of scarlet. This went on for several years, during which time he became more nervous and more tired. He was working too hard and eventually he had a nervous breakdown.

During this time the red had grown in prominence in his aura. Now gray, the color of illness, began to creep into the red, but as he recovered, the gray disappeared and then the blue began to eat up the red. Eventually all the red was consumed and he was well. Nor did he ever afterward wear anything red, scarlet, or maroon.

In another case a woman who ordinarily wore greens and yellows, went to a dress shop which she had patronized for years. The proprietress brought out several dresses but seemed perplexed when the lady tried them on. "I don't know what it is," the proprietress said, "but you need something red or pink. I have never thought you could wear those colors but something in you seems to call for them now." The lady eventually bought a dress with red stripes. Within a month she was in a hospital, suffering from a nervous condition. She recovered, and continued to patronize the same dress shop, but the proprietress never again suggested that she wear red or pink.

9.

TYPES OF AURA

Ursula Roberts

Ursula Roberts is a well-known medium whose work for the Spiritualist Association of Great Britain includes trance sessions and healing.

* * *

To clairvoyant vision the aura appears as a mass of palpitant colour which differs in colouring and size with each individual. It betrays with unerring accuracy the habits, thoughts and diseases of each person. The generous person has an expansive, softly coloured aura. The miser has a murky, contracted aura. The sensualist has a scarlet and crimson field of radiation; the business man, with no thought above worldly success, has an aura of orange tint. The devotee has one of mauve or blue and the saint a dazzling mother-of-pearl light which radiates to a distance of several feet around him. The ordinary person, who is neither very good nor very bad, has an aura of medium size, radiating to a distance of about two feet and showing colouring that is sometimes radiant, sometimes murky, according to their mood.

How do the colours change from the triple foundation of childhood to the multiplicity of adulthood? In childhood the whole aura is volatile; one moment the head colour will be predominant and another the red of the passional nature. The whole nature of childhood is that of flux and change. The adult must of necessity become set in his habit and steady in his thought. He must control the changing moods and learn the art of concentration, by means of which the changing vibrations will become concentrated into certain areas and a bias be made in favour of a certain colour expressive of the predominating traits.

In the case of the business man, whose sole ambition is connected with the promotion of worldly interests, much of his vital power must of necessity become concentrated into the area of the intellect. He is forced to use his mind to think, to plan, to weigh the consequences of every action, with the result that he will develop the head aura to such an extent that it will dominate the emotional aura, and the mixture of yellow and red will result in a bright shade of orange. The man or woman who will give their friendship or affection only if it appeals to their business instincts, will show a vibration similar to this. The saying: "He loves with his head," develops a very literal meaning, since part of the emotional colouring becomes drawn into the head colouring.

The aura of the miser is typical of his nature, in which all the natural instincts are concentrated into the one channel of greed, which is associated with the passional nature. Consequently the aura becomes very small, hard in outline and harsh in colouring. Instead of the vibrations radiating freely around him, they are drawn into one focal centre. All the faculties of the intellect are bent upon the passion of acquisition and in course of time the yellow of the intellect becomes drawn into the red of the passional nature. All the colours are harsh and murky; they combine to form a dirty shade of brownish-orange, while the outer edge of the aura, through being constantly drawn inwards to its centre, ceases to cast off surplus matter and develops what appears as a hard crust, which completely encloses the person. Through this crust it is almost impossible to penetrate, hence the difficulty of reasoning with such a person or of attempting to arouse in them some higher feeling.

The state of such a person is most pitiable, for when we lay down the physical body, consciousness continues within the auric body. If the auric body is encased in a hard shell nobody can break through it to approach him, with the result that the person will suffer intense feelings both of loneliness and helplessness. Nobody can free a person so encased except the person who has created the casing. It behooves us, therefore, for our comfort, not only in this world, but also in the next, to cultivate habits of cheerfulness and of generosity. Let us give freely of our love; our slight knowledge; our personal possessions, if we have any, so that we may develop an aura expanded by love and radiating around us in soft shades of rose-pink, pale blue, lemon or *eau-de-nil*. When we develop broad-mindedness and generosity, the red element in our aura becomes changed to rose-pink. If the person is of a religious nature it changes to blue. The mind aura becomes expanded when we use it to think of other people's needs, and coloured with blue in the amount of love with which we so concern ourselves.

The colour of earthly love is red, being rooted in the sex nature, and the aura of a sensual man or woman is flooded by warm tones of crimson, scarlet and blue. The blue is of a deep rather dirty shade, which at times appears almost purple when mixed with the red. Such a person shows very little intellectual light, because all the powers are focussed in the centre of emotion. They feel, rather than think, and their life is ruled not by reason, but by desire. Sometimes, however, such people conceive strong attachments for their children, or some circumstance arises in which they are forced to curb the desire-nature and love more unselfishly. It is then interesting to notice the gradual shifting of the focus of vibration from the region of the sex organs to the centre of the heart, with a corresponding refinement in colouring. Intense shades of harsh reds change to soft rose and finally to glorious blue.

The intensity with which such people can love when the emotions are transmuted to a higher centre, such as the heart, may in time transform them from sinners into saints; for upon our capacity to love depends our own spiritual advancement. We might say, too, that upon our capacity to love depends the salvation of all humankind, for it is the law that real love must of necessity draw a response from the persons loved, and they in turn will love, becoming also miniature saviours of humankind.

The saints of this world, what of them? The saints who dwell in little slum apartments; the saints of cottages with small backyards and enormous families of children, some of which have been adopted from even less fortunate circumstances? The saints who spend their lives scrubbing, cooking, praying, nursing the infant and the aged; loving everybody indiscriminately, what of them?

I wish you could catch just one glimpse of such an aura, in which all the colours seem to vibrate from the centre of the heart. The red of the passions has been lifted up and changed to flashing shades of azure and sapphire, which interpenetrate what is left of the passional nature, so that it appears mauve, and the colour of the intellect, which plans and thinks for others, is charged with these same shades of blue, so that it appears sometimes as blue, sometimes *eau-de-nil*, sometimes lemon. The glory of such colourings, when perceived in surroundings bereft of beauty and surrounding a person who may be utterly illiterate, makes one feel very humble, for here is a literal example of how the glory of God is attained by merit only and not by wealth, position or knowledge.

Then there are the saints of another world. The saints who give their lives to teach the ignorant; to heal the sick; who grow weary in the service of humanity and who ask no reward except that the mystical grace of God illumine their lives. These people develop an aura wherein the heart and the head centres become equally active. Such persons have studied and attained knowledge to fit them for their tasks; therefore the intellect radiates a glorious glow of yellow which changes to white during moments of extreme exaltation, and lemon or blue in moments of love. Most of the passional nature becomes concentrated into the region of the heart, which vibrates beautiful tones of mauve, purple or blue according to the mood. Auras such as this can only belong to the lovers of humanity, not merely those who serve because they have been trained for a vocation.

Needless to say, every aura differs from another, for one man will love more than another who thinks, and he who thinks may at times love very greatly. It is auras such as these that may eventually expand into the glorious mother-of-pearl of the illumined mahatma, saint or teacher, who will leave such a mark on the history of the world that even the sands of time will have difficulty in effacing it.

With such souls a mysterious moment is attained in which another centre, situated in the top of the head, becomes active and its radiation touches the faint, silvery shell of the casual body, which immediately penetrates the ordinary aura, flooding it with silvery radiance, so that the colours there become luminous with new light and new beauty. The saint becomes not a saint of this world, but a saint of the heavenly world and his or her work, thenceforth, is a work supernal. His or her sojourn in this world is a sojourn of outstanding beauty. It is the attainment not only of a purified consciousness, but of a super-consciousness, and such a person remains for ever a super-man or a super-woman.

10.

THE ETHERIC DOUBLE

Arthur E. Powell

The Theosophical Society was founded in New York in 1875 by Russian-born occultist Helena Petrovina Blavatsky and Henry Steel Olcott, an American. It is today a world-wide organization, with its headquarters in Adyar, Madras, India, devoted to the complete freedom of individual belief in the study of religion, philosophy, and science.

After Blavatsky's death and an intriguing series of struggles on the part of the society for leadership—far too complex to mention here—Annie Besant, a vigorous social reformer (especially for birth control) and Charles Webster Leadbeater, a controversial Church of England clergyman, emerged as directors of the society's activities.

Arthur E. Powell's The Etheric Double, *published in 1925, is primarily a compilation of data published by Besant and Leadbeater over thirty years. In the book's foreword by The Theosophical Research Centre of London's Science Group, we are cautioned to view this work as one based on a clairvoyant perception that one day may be verified, amended, or summarily rejected by new clairvoyant observations and scientific research.*

This selection gives us a detailed look at how man's "inner" structure was viewed by theosophical thought of that time.

* * *

Every student of Occultism is familiar with the fact that man possesses several bodies or vehicles through which he is enabled to express himself on the various planes of nature—physical, astral, mental, and so forth.

The occultist finds that physical matter exists in seven grades or orders of density, viz.:

Atomic.
Sub-Atomic.
Super-Etheric.
Etheric.
Gaseous.
Liquid.
Solid.

Particles of all these grades enter into the composition of the physical vehicle. The latter, however, has two well-marked divisions, viz., the dense body, composed of solids, liquids, and gases, and the Etheric Body, or Double, as it is frequently called, consisting of the four finer grades of physical matter.

Briefly, we shall find that the Etheric Double, while necessary to the life of the physical body, is not, properly speaking, a separate vehicle of consciousness; that it receives and distributes the vital force which emanates from the sun and is thus intimately connected with the physical health; that it possesses certain Chakrams or Force-Centres of its own, each with its distinct function; that upon the action of etheric matter mainly depends the memory of the dream life; that it plays an important part in determining the kind of physical vehicle which an incarnating ego will receive; that, like the physical body, it dies and decays in due course, releasing the "soul" for the next stage in its cyclic journey; that it is especially associated with what is known as Vital or Magnetic Healing, and also with mesmerism, whether for purposes of healing, anaesthesia, or trance; that it is the principal factor concerned in séance-room phenomena, such as the movement of objects, production of "raps" and other sounds, and materialisations of all kinds; that the development of etheric faculties confers new powers and reveals many etheric phenomena, which are beyond the experience of most men; that by the use of the matter of the etheric body objects may be "magnetised," much as living beings may be mesmerised; and, finally, that the etheric body provides the material out of which the substance known as ectoplasm is formed.

The Etheric Double has been given a variety of names. In early Theosophical literature it was often called the astral body, the astral man, or the Linga Sharira. In all later writings, however, none of these terms are ever applied to the Etheric Double, as they belong properly to the body composed of astral matter, the body of Kâma of the Hindus. In reading the Secret Doctrine, therefore, and other books of the older literature, the student must be on his guard not to confuse the two quite distinct bodies, known to-day as the Etheric Double and the Astral Body.

The correct Hindu name for the Etheric Double is Prânamâyakosha, or vehicle of Prâna; in German it is known as the "Doppelgänger"; after death, when separated from the dense physical body, it is known as the "wraith," and has also been called the "phantom," "apparition," or "churchyard ghost." In Râja Yoga the Etheric Double and the dense body together are known as the Sthûlopâdhi, or lowest Upâdhi of Atmâ.

Every solid, liquid, and gaseous particle of the physical body is surrounded with an etheric envelope: hence the Etheric Double, as its name implies, is a perfect duplicate of the dense form. In size it projects about one quarter of an inch beyond the skin. The etheric aura, however, or Health Aura as it is frequently called, projects normally several inches beyond the skin; this will be further described later.

It is important to notice that the dense body and the Etheric Double vary together as to their quality; hence one who sets himself deliberately to purify his dense body, at the same time automatically refines its etheric counterpart.

Into the composition of the Etheric Double must enter

something of all the different grades of etheric matter, but the proportions may vary greatly, and are determined by several factors, such as the race, sub-race, and type of a man, as well as by his individual karma.

In appearance the Etheric Double is a pale violet-grey or blue-grey, faintly luminous, and coarse or fine in texture according as the dense physical body is coarse or fine.

The Etheric Double has two main functions. Firstly, it absorbs Prâna, or Vitality, and distributes this to the whole physical body, as we shall see in detail presently.

Secondly, it acts as an intermediary or bridge between the dense physical body and the astral body, transmitting the consciousness of physical sense-contacts through the etheric brain to the astral body, and also transmitting consciousness from the astral and higher levels down into the physical brain and nervous system.

In addition, the Etheric Double develops within itself certain Centres by means of which the man is able to cognise the etheric world and its hosts of etheric phenomena. These powers or faculties will also be described in due course.

It is important to recognise that the Etheric Double, being merely a part of the physical body, is not normally capable of acting as a separate vehicle of consciousness, in which a man can live or function. It has only a diffused consciousness belonging to its parts, and has no mentality, nor does it readily serve as a medium of mentality, when disjoined from the dense counterpart. As it is a vehicle, not of mental consciousness, but of Prâna or Vitality, its dislocation from the dense particles to which it conveys the life-currents is disturbing and unhealthy. In normal, healthy persons, in fact, the separation of the Etheric Double from the dense body is a matter of difficulty, and the Double is unable to move away from the body to which it belongs.

In persons known as physical or materialising mediums the Double is comparatively easily detachable, and its etheric matter forms the basis of many phenomena of materialisation, which will be dealt with more fully in a later chapter.

The Double may be separated from the dense physical body by accident, death, anaesthetics, such as ether or gas, or mesmerism. The Double being the connecting link between the brain and the higher consciousness, the forcible extrusion of it from the dense physical body by anaesthetics necessarily produces anaesthesia.

Further than this, the etheric matter thus forced out usually wraps itself round the astral body and dulls the consciousness of that vehicle also: hence after the effects of the anaesthetics have worn off there is usually no memory in the brain consciousness of the time spent in the astral vehicle.

The method and consequences of withdrawal of etheric matter by mesmerism will be dealt with more fully in the chapter specially devoted to the purpose.

In conditions of weak health or nervous excitement the Etheric Double may also in great part be extruded from its dense counterpart: the latter then becomes very dully conscious, or entranced, according to the lesser or greater amount of the etheric matter extruded.

Separation of the Double from the dense body is generally accompanied by a considerable decrease of vitality in the latter, the double becoming more vitalised as the energy in the dense body diminishes. In *Posthumous Humanity* Colonel H. S. Olcott says:—

"When the double is projected by a trained expert, even the body seems torpid, and the mind in a 'brown study' or dazed state; the eyes are lifeless in expression, the heart and lung actions feeble and often the temperature much lowered. It is very dangerous to make any sudden noise or burst into the room under such circumstances; for, the double being by instantaneous reaction drawn back into the body, the heart convulsively palpitates, and death even may be caused."

So intimate, in fact, is the connection between the etheric and the dense bodies that an injury inflicted on the Etheric Double will appear as a lesion on the dense body, this being an instance of the curious phenomenon known as repercussion. It is well known that repercussion can also occur in the case of the astral body, an injury to the latter, under certain circumstances, reproducing itself in the physical body.

It seems probable, however, that repercussion can occur only in the case of perfect materialisation, where the form is both visible and tangible, and not when it is (1) tangible though not visible, or (2) visible though not tangible.

It must be borne in mind that the above applies only where matter of the Etheric Double is used for the materialised form. When the materialisation is formed of matter from the circumambient ether, an injury to the form could affect the physical body by repercussion no more than an injury to a marble statue could injure the man himself.

It must also be borne in mind that etheric matter, though invisible to ordinary sight, is still purely physical, and can therefore be affected by cold and heat, and also by powerful acids.

Persons who have lost a limb by amputation sometimes complain that they can feel pain at the extremities of the amputated limb, *i.e.*, at the place where the limb used to be.

This is due to the fact that the etheric portion of the limb is not removed with the dense physical portion, but can still be seen in its place by clairvoyant sight, and therefore, under suitable stimulus, sensations can be aroused in his etheric limb and transmitted to the consciousness.

There are certain circumstances in which it is both permissible and desirable to form either a shell or a shield of etheric matter, to protect oneself or other people from unpleasant influences of various kinds.

Thus, for example, in a mixed crowd there is quite likely to be present some physical magnetism distasteful, if not positively injurious, to a student of Occultism. Some persons, also, being themselves low in vitality, have the faculty, usually unconscious, of depleting others in their vicinity of their stores of Prâna. Provided these vampirelike people took from others only those etheric particles which are normally expelled from the body as not needed, no harm would be done, but often the suction is so intense that the whole circulation of Prâna in the victim is hastened, the rose-coloured particles also being drawn out of the system before their Prânic content has been assimilated by their owner. A capable vampire can thus drain a person of all his strength in a few minutes.

The vampire is not appreciably benefited by the vitality of which he has robbed others, because his own system tends to dissipate what he acquires without proper assimilation. A person in this condition needs mesmeric treatment, strictly limited quantities of Prâna being supplied to him, until the elasticity of his Etheric Double is restored, so that both the suction and the leakage cease. The leakage of vitality takes place through every pore of the body rather than through any one portion of it.

In certain abnormal cases another entity may attempt to seize and obsess the physical bodies of others. Or, again, it may be necessary to sleep, e.g., in a railway carriage, in close physical proximity with people of the vampire type or whose emanations are coarse and undesirable; or the student may have to visit persons or places where disease is rampant.

Some people are so sensitive that they are apt to reproduce in their own bodies the symptoms of others who are weak or diseased; others, again, suffer considerably from the incessant play of the multiplex vibrations in a noisy city.

In all these cases an etheric shell may be utilised with advantage to protect oneself. It is important to note, however, that an etheric shell which keeps *out* etheric matter will also keep it *in*, and that therefore one's own etheric emanations, many of which are poisonous, will be kept within the shell.

The shell is made by an effort of will and imagination.

It may be done in two ways. Either the periphery of the etheric aura, which follows the shape of and is slightly larger than the physical body, may be densified, or an ovoid shell of etheric matter may be manufactured out of the surrounding atmosphere. The latter is preferable, though it demands a far greater exertion of the will and a more definite knowledge of the way in which physical matter is moulded by it.

Students who wish to guard their physical bodies during sleep by means of an etheric shell must be careful to make the latter of etheric, not astral, matter. A case is recorded of a student who made this mistake, with the consequence that the physical body was left entirely unprotected, while he himself floated away in an impenetrable astral shell which permitted nothing to pass either to or from the consciousness imprisoned within.

The formation of an etheric shell before going to sleep may be of assistance in helping the experiences of the Ego to come through into the waking consciousness by preventing the thoughts which are always floating in the etheric world, and constantly bombarding the vehicles, from entering into the sleeping etheric brain and becoming there mixed up with the thoughts of that etheric brain itself.

The etheric part of the brain, being the playground of the creative imagination, takes an active part in dreams, especially those caused by impressions from outside, or from any internal pressure from the cerebral vessels. Its dreams are usually dramatic, for it draws on the accumulated contents of the physical brain, and arranges, dissociates, and recombines these after its own fancies, thus creating the lower world of dream.

The best method of remaining, whilst awake, practically impervious to the impingement of thought from without is to keep the brain fully employed instead of leaving it idle, the door wide open for the streams of inconsequent chaos to pour into it.

In sleep the etheric part of the brain is of course even

more at the mercy of outside thought-currents. By the means suggested above the student should be able to keep himself free from such troubles.

In some cases it is not necessary to make a shell to surround the whole body, but merely a small local shield to guard oneself against a special contact.

Thus some sensitive people suffer acutely merely from shaking hands with others. In such cases a temporary shield of etheric matter may be formed, by an effort of will and imagination, which will completely protect the hand and arm from the entry of a single particle charged with undesirable magnetism.

Similar shields are used for protection against fire, though for this purpose a far greater knowledge of practical magic is needed. Such shields of etheric matter, the thinnest layer of which can be so manipulated as to be absolutely impervious to heat, may be spread over the hands, the feet, or over the hot stones or other substances used in the fire-walking ceremonies still practised in certain parts of the world. This phenomenon is occasionally seen at spiritual séances, the sitters being enabled to handle red-hot coals with impunity.

11

THE HEALTH AURA

Charles Webster Leadbeater

In this selection from **Man Visible and Invisible,** *which has become a best-selling theosophical classic, and required reading for researchers studying the aura, Leadbeater explains the "invisible" nature of the vital force and its influence on life and health.*

* * *

Much of physical matter which is seen by clairvoyant sight to be part of the aura of man is in the etheric state, and constitutes what is often called the Etheric Double. This is not in any sense a separate vehicle, but must be considered simply as part of the physical body. It is clearly visible to the clairvoyant as a mass of faintly luminous violet-grey mist, interpenetrating the denser part of the physical body, and extending very slightly beyond it. This etheric matter is the link between the astral and the physical, but it has also a very important function as the vehicle of the vital force on the physical plane.

This vital force is poured upon us from the sun, which is the source of life in this inner sense as well as by means of its light and heat in the outer world. The earth's atmosphere is full of this force at all times, though it is in special activity in brilliant sunlight; and it is only by absorbing it that our physical bodies are able to live. The absorption of this vital energy is one of the functions of the etheric part of that organ which we call the spleen; and that organ possesses the curious property of specializing and transmuting the force as it passes through it, so that it presents a totally different appearance.

The force itself is naturally invisible, like all other forces; but as it exists around us in the atmosphere it clothes itself in millions of tiny particles which are colorless though intensely active. After it has been absorbed into the human body through the spleen, however, these particles take on a beautiful pale rose-color, and they flow in a constant stream over and through the whole body along the nerves, in the same manner as the blood-corpuscles flow along the arteries and veins, the brain being the centre of this nervous circulation. . . .

It is evident that this flow is necessary to the proper working of the nerves, for when it is withdrawn there is no sensation. We know how a limb may be so numbed by cold as to be absolutely insensible to the touch; and the reason of such insensibility is that the vital force is no longer flowing through it. It might be supposed that it was rather due to the failure of the circulation of the blood, but those who have studied mesmerism are aware that one of the commonest experiments is to produce similar insensibility in a limb by magnetic passes. This does not at all interfere with the circulation of the blood, for the limb remains warm; but it does check the circulation of the subject's life-fluid, and substitutes for it that of the magnetizer. The nerves of the subject are still there, and (so far as physical sight can see) in perfect working order; yet they do not perform their office of reporting to his brain, because the fluid which animates them is not connected with that brain, but with the brain of the operator.

In a healthy man the spleen does its work in so generous a fashion that the specialized life-force is present in very large quantities, and is constantly radiating from the body in all directions. A man in perfect health, therefore, not only is able to impart some of it to another intentionally, but is also constantly though unconsciously shedding strength and vitality on those around him. On the other hand, a man who from weakness or other causes is unable to specialize for his own use a sufficient amount of the world's life-force, sometimes, equally unconsciously, acts as a sponge and absorbs the already specialized vitality of any sensitive person who is unfortunate enough to come into contact with him, to his own temporary benefit, no doubt, but often to the injury of his victim. Probably most people have experienced this in minor degree, and have found that there is someone among their acquaintances after whose visits they always feel a quite unaccountable weariness and languor; and a similar lassitude is frequently felt by persons who attend spiritualistic séances without taking special precautions against the drain upon their vital force set up in the course of the manifestations.

This radiation produces a striking effect upon the appearance of what we may call the purely physical part of the man's aura. It is well known that tiny particles of dense physical matter are constantly being thrown off from man's body, in insensible perspiration and in other ways; and these particles also are visible to clairvoyant sight as a faint grey mist. These particles are in many cases crystals, and therefore are seen in certain geometrical forms; for example, the tiny cubes of sodium chloride or common salt, are among the most frequent. This purely physical part of man's surrounding is sometimes called the health-aura, from the fact that its condition is greatly affected by the health of the body from which it emanates. It is a faint bluish-white, almost colorless, and has the appearance of being striated; that is, it is full of, or perhaps it might rather be said to be composed of, an infinitude of straight lines radiating evenly in all directions from the pores of the body. That at least is the normal condition of these lines when the body is in perfect health; they are separate, orderly, and as nearly parallel as their radiation allows. But on the advent of disease there is an instant change, the lines in the neighborhood of the part affected becoming erratic, and lying about in all directions in the wildest confusion, or drooping like the stems of faded flowers.

The reasons for this curious appearance is itself an

interesting one. We find that the rigidity and parallelism of the lines of this health-aura are caused by the constant radiation of life-force from the healthy body; and as soon as this radiation ceases, the lines fall into the confused condition described above. As the patient recovers, the normal radiation of this magnetic form of vital energy is gradually resumed, and the lines of the health-aura are thereby combed into order once more. As long as the lines are firm and straight, and the force steadily radiates between them, the body seems to be almost entirely protected from the attack of evil physical influences, such as germs of disease, for example—such germs being repelled and carried away by the outrush of the life-force; but when from any cause—through weakness, through wound or injury, through over-fatigue, through extreme depression of spirits, or through the excesses of an irregular life—an unusually large amount of vitality is required to repair damage or waste within the body, and there is consequently a serious diminution in the quantity radiated, this system of defence becomes dangerously weak, and it is comparatively easy for the deadly germs to effect an entrance.

It may also be mentioned that it is possible by an effort of will to check this radiation of vitality at the outer extremity of its lines, and there to build it into a kind of wall or shell, which will be absolutely impervious to these germs—and, with a little further effort, impervious also to any kind of astral or elemental influence—so long as such effort of the will is maintained.

12.

THE ASTRAL BODY

Sylvan Muldoon and
Hereward Carrington

Sylvan Muldoon, who began to have "out of body experiences" in his early teens, teams up here with psychic researcher Hereward Carrington to describe the nature of "astral projection."

* * *

The belief that man possesses a "double" or spiritual body of some kind dates back to the veriest antiquity. In the Egyptian *Book of the Dead*, this idea is already fully developed, and illustrated in considerable detail, where the Ka is shown returning to its mummified body. In China and Tibet the same doctrine held sway from time immemorial, and ancient Chinese prints show the emergence of such a body, when a victim is being subjected to torture. The ancient writings of Tibet enter into the question at great length. Among primitives, this belief has always been held—that a man, during his sleep, leaves his physical body and wanders far afield.

The belief in some sort of spiritual body has doubtless been maintained and fortified, throughout history, by constantly reported cases of *apparitions*; or, more popularly speaking, "ghosts." It is perhaps hardly necessary to emphasize the fact that such cases have been recounted from the earliest times, and from every country in the world. Until our own times, "ghosts" were unceremoniously classified under one of two categories: they were dismissed as hallucinations and the disordered imaginations of credulous minds, *or* they were accepted as real, outstanding entities—that is, space-occupying forms. Holding such diametrically opposite views, it is small wonder that believers and disbelievers could find no common ground on which to meet. Such ground was only provided by the progress of psychic science, and the later and more rational interpretation of the majority of such phantoms.

Briefly, the modern view is that the majority of apparitions are indeed subjective, rather than objective, but that, in many instances, they are more than this. If the appearance of the phantom coincides with the death or illness of its originator, we seem forced to the conclusion that some causal connection exists between the death and the appearance of the phantasm; and this factor is now thought to be *telepathy*. Accordingly, such cases are now generally regarded, for the most part, as "telepathic hallucinations." The mind of the dying person has in some manner influenced the mind of the seer, causing it to conjure up the visual picture of that person, which becomes "externalized" in the form of a hallucination. In some such way, doubtless, the vast majority of "apparitions of the dying" may be explained.

But not all of them! Obstinate cases keep cropping up which seemingly cannot be accounted for in this simple manner. Some "ghosts" are reported to have opened and closed doors, or pulled aside curtains, or produced raps, or been seen by animals, or by several people at the same time. Occasionally, such "ghosts" have been photographed. A hallucination cannot snuff a candle or open a door, or affect the emulsion on a photographic plate! That requires some semi-material body, capable of influencing matter.

We desire to deal with those rare cases where there seems to be evidence of the objectivity of the phantom observed; or, more specifically, of those instances in which the projector has not only been *seen*—but has *been* the phantom! These are the cases of so-called "astral projections," in which the subject is actually conscious of his presence, and aware of the fact that he has left his physical body. In such cases, he does not *see* the ghost, he *is* the ghost!

Years ago, students of psychic science pointed out the fact that the majority of apparitions were fleeting and evanescent; they merely appeared and disappeared without rhyme or reason, and conveyed no information of importance. This is precisely what we should expect if the phantasms were merely "telepathic hallucinations." Since they have no intrinsic reality, they have no mind of their own. As Homer said, "There is no *heart* in them."

But, in cases of astral projection, all this is completely reversed. The phantom is then intensely aware of its own personal identity and active consciousness. It has a mind of its own, and realizes very fully that it is there in person—its main difficulty being in making others sense its presence. Here, then, is one of the main distinguishing characteristics between these two types of phenomena. The average "ghost" has no mind of its own, seeming to be a mere unconscious projection of the mind of another. The astral phantom, on the other hand, *has* a mind of its own, and possesses an active, wide-awake consciousness which—to those who have experienced astral projection—is certain, and in no wise resembles dream-consciousness. This fact is emphasized over and over again by our correspondents, and is fully borne out by my own personal experiences. The consciousness which one maintains in astral projection is the same as the waking consciousness, and is entirely different from the *sort* of consciousness one has in dreams. . . .

So much for the mind animating the phantom. What about the composition of the spiritual body itself? Certainly it is not composed of ordinary matter, for if it were it would be palpable to our senses, and differ in no essential way from our physical bodies. Nor can it be entirely immaterial or spiritual, in the usual meaning of the word, for if it were it would be incapable of being seen or sensed by any of our normal sensory faculties—as it certainly *is* when the phantom form is perceived. This being granted, we can only assume that the astral body is composed of some semi-material constituents, too subtle for ordinary sense-registration, of a nature termed "fluidic" by the magnetists and by many students of the occult.

It is true that this is, in a way, very vague and in a sense "unscientific." Traditional science does not recognize the existence of any such half-way-house substance; a body must be either material or non-material! However, late discoveries in physics have made scientific men far more cautious and far less dogmatic than they were a few years ago. They are now inclined to believe that matter possesses many mysterious properties hitherto undreamed of, and that, in the last analysis, it represents nothing more than bundles of energy. . . . Furthermore, it is quite possible for us to suppose that the degree of materiality of such a body varies from time to time, and under different conditions; that it may become more solid, as it were, for a brief time, while manifesting, becoming less material immediately afterwards. We have the analogy of materializations to guide us here, which have been observed in séances. In these cases a hand (for example) becomes sufficiently material to be seen and even touched by those present, for a few seconds, and immediately thereafter impalpable to the senses of sight and touch. We have other analogies to guide us here too.

A fog, for example, is caused by the adhesion of tiny particles of soot to the droplets of water suspended in a moisture-laden atmosphere. When this occurs the fog becomes very noticeable, and may become so dense as to shut off the view of distant and even near-by objects. With the evaporation of the water the "fog" disappears. Experiments have been tried by certain occult students in the creation and projection of so-called "thought-forms," which are ordinarily invisible (though real) but which can be made visible by means of steam or the smoke rising from burning incense. The picture we might form in our minds here is that the hand, say normally impalpable, becomes visible when plunged into material which renders it visible for the time being—much as the fog becomes visible under suitable conditions. As soon as these conditions cease to exist, the invading substance immediately becomes invisible again.

This is, of course, a crude analogy, but may perhaps help us to understand what happens at such times, and how—to our senses—the same essential constituents may be at the same time material and immaterial. . . . To illustrate this point more clearly, we may refer to an incident in one of Sir William Crookes's séances with D. D. Home, in which some spectators saw a bunch of flowers being transported from one side of the room to the other; some sitters saw a cloudlike mass attached to the flowers, while others saw a distinct hand, which was seemingly carrying the flowers across the room. Here, obviously, the hand was just on the borderline of visibility, perceived by those most sensitive, partially perceived by those less so, and totally unperceived by those whose sensitivity was wholly lacking. We might justly conclude, it seems to us, that many astral bodies and phantom forms fall into this same category; and this seems to be further borne out by the varied testimonies of people residing in "haunted houses." Some see the forms while others do not.

If matter, in the last analysis, is energy, and if thought is dynamic, so that it too must be an expression of energy (in the psycho-physical sense—that is, as the "correlate" of thought) then it may be that the creative energy of the mind may have much to do with the degree of substantiality of such a body, during the time of its actual manifestation. . . .

The degree of materiality of the astral body would thus vary and fluctuate according to the density of the visualized will of the subject—just as the famous medium Eusapia Palladino was wont to say that she could move material objects in her environment if her will were sufficiently *solid*. It is undoubtedly difficult for us to understand precisely what is meant by these cryptic statements, but we are dealing here with subtle problems, and must do the best we can to read between the lines—trusting that the psychic science of the future will throw an increasing light upon these difficult questions!

The existence of man's spiritual body is confirmed by a variety of psychic phenomena—varying greatly in the degree of their cogency. First, there is the massive weight of human belief and testimony, from the earliest times to our own day, in all parts of the world, and among civilized and uncivilized peoples. Second, we have those cases of apparitions in which the phantom-form seems to exhibit a mind and will of its own—often imparting information unknown to the seer at the time, but afterwards verified. Third, we have those cases in which material effects are apparently produced by the phantom, or its image appears upon photographic plates. Fourth, we have instances of materialization, at séances, witnessed in the presence of reputable mediums, such as Home, Palladino, and many others. Fifth, we have cases of astral projection, in which the subject sees his own phantom body, and is occasionally seen by others. In these last instances, especially, we have evidence that the phantom form possesses a mind of its own, separate and distinct from the physical brain and body, which latter may be seen resting upon the bed. The cumulative mass of such testimony is, we submit, most impressive, and gives us the right to believe that such a "spiritual body" exists—as St. Paul long ago stated.

Successful astral projection is based upon this fundamental conception: that the "double"—the etheric counterpart of man—is capable at times of being detached from the physical body, carrying with it the consciousness of the subject, so that he now lives *in* that body, and is often enabled to look back upon his physical body, asleep upon the bed, and observe it as an "outsider". . . . Connecting these two bodies—the astral and the physical—is an ethereal cord, usually emerging from the forehead of the physical and entering the astral at the back of the neck. So long as this cord is intact, life is present, and the astral body eventually returns to reanimate the physical organism. When, however, this cord is severed (as it is at death) then the astral body can no longer return to reanimate the body, which then disintegrates.

Such detachments or projections are usually spontaneous or involuntary—especially at first. But later the subject may be enabled to produce such projections experimentally, and then there is opened up to him a vast field for study, fascinating in the extreme! Once one has had an experience of this kind, he knows that he is a living soul, and that death is nothing, no longer holding the terrors which were formally associated with it. For does he not know that he is able to live and function, quite apart from the gross physical body? Death is nothing more than the *permanent* separation of the two bodies, which he has *temporarily* separated many times before; or, as Myers expressed it, "Death is but the irrevocable projection of the human spirit". . . .

We live in an intensely sceptical, practical age, and the average man in the street would probably ridicule any such notion as "sheer nonsense". . . . Once he has had an experience of the kind, however, his opinion changes! But it is true, of course, that the *average* man does not have any such experience, and he is inclined to accept and believe only what his senses confirm. If we can see and feel and touch a thing, he believes in its "reality"; if he cannot, he is inclined to put it down to illusion and hallucination.

Of course such an attitude typifies a closed mind, and is exactly the reverse of the truth. Modern Science has brought home to us the fact that *the invisible is the real*; that whatever the senses can perceive are *phenomena*, merely, and that all the energies and realities of the universe are and for ever remain invisible. Consciousness is the greatest reality there is; yet it has never been perceived by any of the ordinary senses. The average man thinks of himself as a body, possessing a temporary mind; the truth of the matter is that man is a spirit, possessing a temporary body. The importance of this realization need hardly be emphasized. It gives us a true perspective of man, in his relation to the Cosmos. And it is important to emphasize the point that this realization has been brought about, in many instances, by the experience of conscious astral projection, which then assumed the same relative importance in his life as a "cosmic conscious" experience would in the life of a mystic. . . . Many regard it as too sacred to be discussed. Fortunately, there are others who regard such an experience from the scientific point of view, and are profoundly interested in ascertaining what has happened. . . .

13.

NOT WITH A WAND,
NOR LIGHTLY

Robert A. Monroe

This selection is a modern and very personal account of a man who began to have "out of body" experiences. It stresses his initial confusion about and gradual acceptance of this phenomena.

* * *

In the spring of 1958 I was living a reasonably normal life with a reasonably normal family. Because we appreciated nature and quiet, ours was a country environment. The only unorthodox activity was my experimentation with techniques of data learning during sleep—with myself as the chief subject.

The first sign of deviation from the norm took place on a Sunday afternoon. While the rest of the family had gone to church, I conducted an experiment by listening to a particular tape recording in a highly isolated environment. It was a simple attempt to force concentration on a single intelligent-signal source (aural) with lowered signal input from the other senses. Degree of retention and recall would indicate the success of the technique.

Isolated from other sights and sounds, I listened to the tape. It contained no unusual or stray suggestion. Most significant in retrospect was the strong suggestion to remember and recall all that took place during the relaxation exercise. The tape ran its course with no unusual result. My recall was thorough and complete because it had been a product of my own efforts and thus familiar to me. Perhaps too much so, as no retention and recall of original or new material was possible in my case. The technique would have to be utilized with some other subject.

When my family returned, we all had brunch, which consisted of scrambled eggs, bacon, and coffee. Some unimportant controversy occurred at the table, which was not germane to the problem.

A little over an hour later, I was seized with a severe, iron-hard cramp which extended across my diaphragm or solar plexus area just under my rib cage. It was a solid band of unyielding ache.

At first, I thought it was some form of food poisoning from brunch. In desperation, I forced myself to regurgitate, but my stomach was empty. Other members of my family who had eaten the same food showed no signs of illness or discomfort. I tried exercising and walking, on the assumption that it was a cramped abdominal muscle. It was not appendicitis, as my appendix had been removed. I could breathe properly in spite of the pain, and my heart appeared normal in pulse rate. There was no perspiration or other symptoms whatsoever—just the hard, tense, locked-in-place rigidity of a band of muscles in the upper abdomen.

It occurred to me that perhaps some factor in the recording had caused it. In going over the tape and the written copy from which it had been made, I found nothing unusual. What suggestion there was, I complied with, seeking to relieve any unconscious suggestion that might have been applied. Still, no relief.

Perhaps I should have phoned immediately for a doctor. However, it didn't seem that serious, nor did it become any worse. But it didn't get any better, either. Finally, we did phone for medical help. All of the local doctors were away or playing golf.

From one-thirty in the afternoon until around midnight, the cramp and pain continued. No typical home medication seemed to alleviate it. Sometime after twelve I fell asleep from pure exhaustion.

I woke up in the early morning, and the cramp and pain were gone. There was muscle soreness throughout the afflicted area, much as one gets from overcoughing, but no more. What caused the cramp in this area is still unknown. It is mentioned only because it was the first out-of-the-ordinary event, physical or otherwise, that took place.

In retrospect, perhaps it was the touch of a magic wand, or a sledge hammer, although I didn't know it at the time.

Some three weeks later, the second major event entered the picture. There had been no further recorded tape experimentation, because the suspicion was strong that the cramp was somehow related. Thus there was nothing that apparently triggered the event.

Again, it was a Sunday afternoon and the family had gone to church. I lay down on the couch in the living room for a short nap while the house was quiet. I had just become prone (head to the north, if that had any meaning), when a beam or ray seemed to come out of the sky to the north at about a 30° angle from the horizon. It was like being struck by a warm light. Only this was daylight and no beam was visible, if there truly was one.

I thought it *was* sunlight at first, although this was impossible on the north side of the house. The effect when the beam struck my entire body was to cause it to shake violently or "vibrate." I was utterly powerless to move. It was as if I were being held in a vise.

Shocked and frightened, I forced myself to move. It was like pushing against invisible bonds. As I slowly sat upright on the couch, the shaking and vibration slowly faded away and I was able to move freely.

I stood up and walked around. There had been no loss of consciousness that I was aware of, and the clock showed that only a few seconds had elapsed since I had stretched out on the couch. I had not closed my eyes, and had seen the room and heard outdoor noises during the entire episode. I looked out the window, especially to the north, although why and what I expected to see, I don't know. Everything looked normal and serene. I went outside for a walk to puzzle over this strange thing that had happened.

Within the following six weeks, the same peculiar condition manifested itself nine times. It occurred at different periods and locales, and the only common factor was that it began just after I had lain down for rest or sleep. Whenever it took place, I fought myself to a sitting position, and the "shaking" faded away. Although my body "felt" the shaking, I could see no visible evidence that it was doing so.

My limited knowledge of medicine envisioned many possibilities as the cause. I thought of epilepsy, but I understood that epileptics had no memory or sensation in such seizures. Furthermore, I understood that epilepsy is hereditary and shows signs at an early age, and neither was evident in my case.

Second was the possibility of a brain disorder such as a tumor or growth. Again, the symptoms were not typical, but this could be it. With trepidation, I went to our longtime family physician, Dr. Richard Gordon, and explained the symptoms. As an internist and diagnostician, he should have had what answers there may have been. He also knew my medical history, such as it was.

After a thorough physical, Dr. Gordon suggested that I had been working too hard, that I get more sleep and take off a little weight. In short, he could find nothing wrong with me physically. He laughed at the possibility of a brain tumor or epilepsy. I took his word for it and returned home relieved.

If there was no physical basis for the phenomenon, I thought, it must be hallucinatory, a form of dreaming. Therefore, if the condition came again, I would observe it as objectively as possible. It obliged by "coming on" that very evening.

It began some two minutes after I lay down to sleep. This time, I was determined to stay with it and see what happened rather than fight my way out of it. As I lay there, the "feeling" surged into my head and swept over my entire body. It was not a shaking, but more of a "vibration," steady and unvarying in frequency. It felt much like an electric shock running through the entire body without the pain involved. Also, the frequency seemed somewhat below the sixty-cycle pulsation, perhaps half that rate.

Frightened, I stayed with it, trying to remain calm. I could still see the room around me, but could hear little above the roaring sound caused by the vibrations. I wondered what would happen next.

Nothing happened. After some five minutes, the sensation slowly faded away and I got up feeling perfectly normal. My pulse rate was up, evidently due to the excitement, but no more. With this result, I lost much of my fear of the condition.

In the next four or five occurrences of the vibration, I discovered little more. On one occasion, at least, it seemed to develop into a ring of sparks about two feet in diameter, with the axis of my body in the center of the ring. I could actually see this ring if I closed my eyes. The ring would start at the head and slowly sweep down to my toes and back to the head, keeping this up in a regular oscillation. The time of the cycle seemed to be some five seconds. As the ring passed over each section of my body, I could feel the vibrations like a band cutting through that section. When the ring passed over my head, a great roaring surged with it, and I felt the vibrations in my brain. I attempted to study this flaming electrical-seeming ring, but could discover no reason for it, or what it was.

All of this remained unknown to my wife and children. I could see no reason to worry or concern them until something definite was known of it. I did take a friend into my confidence, a well-known psychologist, Dr. Foster Bradshaw. If it had not been for him, I cannot predict where I would be at this time. Perhaps in an institution.

I discussed the matter with him, and he was most interested. He suggested it might be some form of hallucination. Like Dr. Gordon, he knew me well. Consequently, he laughed at the concept that I was in the beginning stages of schizophrenia or the like. I asked him what he thought I should do. I shall always remember his answer.

"Why, there's nothing else you can do but look into it and see what it is," Dr. Bradshaw replied. "Anyhow, it doesn't seem you have much choice. If it happened to me, I'd go off in the woods somewhere and keep trying until I found the answer."

The difference was that it was happening to me and not to Dr. Bradshaw, and I couldn't afford to go off in the woods, either literally or figuratively. I had a family to support, among other things.

Several months passed, and the vibration condition continued to occur. It almost became boring, until late one night when I was lying in bed just before sleep. The vibrations came and I wearily and patiently waited for them to pass away so I could go to sleep. As I lay there, my arm was draped over the right side of the bed, fingers just brushing the rug.

Idly, I tried to move my fingers and found I could scratch the rug. Without thinking or realizing that I *could* move my fingers during the vibration, I pushed with the tips of my fingers against the rug. After a moment's resistance, my fingers seemed to penetrate the rug and touch the floor underneath. With mild curiosity, I pushed my hand down farther. My fingers went through the floor and there was the rough upper surface of the ceiling of the room below. I felt around, and there was a small triangular chip of wood, a bent nail, and some sawdust. Only mildly interested in this daydream sensation, I pushed my hand still deeper. It went through the first-floor ceiling and I felt as if my whole arm was through the floor. My hand touched water. Without excitement, I splashed the water with my fingers.

Suddenly, I became fully aware of the situation. I was wide awake. I could see the moonlit landscape through the window. I could feel myself lying on the bed, the covers over my body, the pillow under my head, my chest rising and falling as I breathed. The vibrations were still present, but to a lesser degree.

Yet, impossibly, my hand was playing in a pool of water, and my arm felt as if it was stuck down through the floor. I was surely wide awake and the sensation was still there. How could I be awake in all other respects and still "dream" that my arm was stuck down through the floor?

The vibrations started to fade, and for some reason I thought there was a connection between my arm stuck through the floor and their presence. If they faded away before I got my arm "out," the floor might close in and I would lose an arm. Perhaps the vibrations had made a hole in the floor temporarily. I didn't stop to consider the "how" of it.

I yanked my arm out of the floor, pulled it up on the bed, and the vibrations ended soon after. I got up, turned on the light, and looked at the spot beside the bed. There was no hole in the floor or rug. They were just as they always had been. I looked at my hand and arm, and even looked for the water on my hand. There was none, and my arm seemed perfectly normal. I looked about the room. My wife was sleeping quietly in the bed, nothing seemed amiss.

I thought about the hallucination for a long time before I was able to calm down enough to sleep. The next day I considered actually cutting a hole in the floor to see if what I had felt was there on the subfloor—the triangular chip of wood, the bent nail, and the sawdust. At the time, I couldn't see disfiguring the floor because of a wild hallucination.

I told Dr. Bradshaw of this episode, and he agreed that it was a rather convincing daydream. He was in favor of cutting the hole in the floor to find out what was there. He introduced me to Dr. Lewis Wolberg, a psychiatrist of note. At a dinner party, I casually mentioned the vibration phenomenon to Dr. Wolberg. He was only politely interested, and evidently in no mood for "business," for which I couldn't blame him. I didn't have the courage to ask him about the arm in the floor.

It was becoming fairly confusing. My environment and personal experience had led me to expect some kind of answers or at least promising opinions from modern technology. I had an above-normal scientific, engineering, and medical background as a layman. Now, I was faced with something where answers or even extrapolation was not quickly available. In retrospect, I still cannot envisage having dropped the matter entirely at any time. It may be that I could not have done so if I tried.

If I thought I faced incongruities at this point, it was because I did not know what was yet to come. Some four weeks later, when the "vibrations" came again, I was duly cautious about attempting to move an arm or leg. It was late at night, and I was lying in bed before sleep. My wife had fallen asleep beside me. There was a surge that seemed to be in my head, and quickly the condition spread through my body. It all seemed the same. As I lay there trying to decide how to analyze the thing in another way, I just happened to think how nice it would be to take a glider up and fly the next afternoon (my hobby at that time). Without considering any consequences—not knowing there would be any—I thought of the pleasure it would bring.

After a moment, I became aware of something pressing against my shoulder. Half-curious, I reached back and up to feel what it was. My hand encountered a smooth wall. I moved my hand along the wall the length of my arm and it continued smooth and unbroken.

My senses fully alert, I tried to see in the dim light. It *was* a wall, and I was lying against it with my shoulder. I immediately reasoned that I had gone to sleep and fallen out of bed. (I had never done so before, but all sorts of strange things were happening, and falling out of bed was quite possible.)

Then I looked again. Something was wrong. This wall had no windows, no furniture against it, no doors. It was not a wall in my bedroom. Yet somehow it was familiar. Identification came instantly. It wasn't a wall, it was the ceiling. I was floating against the ceiling, bouncing gently with any movement I made. I rolled in the air, startled, and looked down. There, in the dim light below me, was the bed. There were two figures lying in the bed. To the right was my wife. Beside her was someone else. Both seemed asleep.

This was a strange dream, I thought. I was curious. Whom would I dream to be in bed with my wife? I looked more closely, and the shock was intense. I was the someone on the bed!

My reaction was almost instantaneous. Here I was, there was my body. I was dying, this was death, and I wasn't ready to die. Somehow, the vibrations were killing me. Desperately, like a diver, I swooped down to my body and dove in. I then felt the bed and the covers, and when I opened my eyes, I was looking at the room from the perspective of my bed.

What had happened? Had I truly almost died? My heart was beating rapidly, but not unusually so. I moved my arms and legs. Everything seemed normal. The vibrations had faded away. I got up and walked around the room, looked out the window, smoked a cigarette.

It was a long time before I had the courage to return to bed, lie down, and try to sleep.

The following week I returned to Dr. Gordon for another physical examination. I didn't tell him the reason for the visit, but he could see I was worried. He carefully examined me, ran blood tests, fluoroscopes, electrocardiograms, palpated all cavities, ran urinalysis, and about everything else he could think of. He checked very carefully for indications of brain lesions, and asked me many questions relating to motor action of various parts of the body. He arranged for an EEG (brain-wave analysis), which evidently showed no unusual problem. At least he never reported any to me, and I am sure he would have.

Dr. Gordon gave me some tranquilizers, and sent me home with orders to take off weight, smoke less, get more rest—and said that if I had a problem, it was not a physical one.

I met with Dr. Bradshaw, my psychologist friend. He

was even less helpful and far from sympathetic when I told him the story. He thought I should try to repeat the experience if I could. I told him I wasn't ready to die.

"Oh, I don't think you'll do that," Dr. Bradshaw stated calmly. "Some of the fellows who practice yoga and those Eastern religions claim they can do it whenever they want to."

I asked him "do" what.

"Why, get out of the physical body for awhile," he replied. "They claim they can go all over the place. You ought to try it."

I told him that was ridiculous. Nobody can travel around without their physical body.

"Well, I wouldn't be too sure," Dr. Bradshaw replied calmly. "You ought to read something about the Hindus. Did you study any philosophy in college?"

I said I had, but there was nothing I could recall about this traveling-without-the-body business.

"Maybe you didn't have the right philosophy professor, that's what it seems to me." Dr. Bradshaw lit a cigar, then looked at me. "Well, don't be so closed-minded. Try it and find out. As *my* old philosophy professor said, 'If you're blind in one eye, turn your head, and if you're blind in both eyes, then open your ears and listen.' "

I asked what to do if you were deaf, too, but I didn't get a reply.

Of course, Dr. Bradshaw had every reason to be casual about it. It was happening to me, not him. I don't know what I would have done without his pragmatic approach and his wonderful sense of humor. It is a debt I shall never be able to repay.

The vibrations came and went six more times before I got up the courage to try to repeat the experience. When I did, it was an anticlimax. With the vibrations in full force, I thought of floating upward—and I did.

I smoothly floated up over the bed, and when I willed myself to stop, I did, floating in mid-air. It was not a bad feeling at all, but I was nervous about falling suddenly. After a few seconds I thought myself downward, and a moment later I felt myself in bed again with all normal physical senses fully operating. There had been no discontinuity in consciousness from the moment I lay down in bed until I got up after the vibrations faded. If it wasn't real—just a hallucination or dream—I was in trouble. I couldn't tell where wakefulness stopped and dreaming began.

There are thousands of people in mental institutions who have just that problem.

The second time I attempted to disassociate deliberately, I was successful. Again I went up to ceiling height. However, this time I experienced an overwhelmingly strong sexual drive and could think of nothing else. Embarrassed and irritated at myself because of my inability to control this tide of emotion, I returned back into my physical body.

It wasn't until some five episodes later that I discovered the secret of such control. The evident importance of sexuality in the whole subject is great. At the time, it was an exasperating mental block which held me within the confines of the room where my physical body lay.

With no other applicable terminology, I began to call the condition the Second State, and the other, non-physical body we seem to possess the Second Body. So far this terminology fits as well as anything else.

It wasn't until the first evidential experience which could be checked that I seriously considered these to be anything but daydreams, hallucinations, a neurotic aberration, the beginnings of schizophrenia, fantasies caused by self-hypnosis, or worse.

That first evidential experience was indeed a sledge-hammer blow. If I accepted the data as fact, it struck hard at nearly all of my life experience to that date, my training, my concepts, and my sense of values. Most of all, it shattered my faith in the totality and certainty of our culture's scientific knowledge. I was sure our scientists had all the answers. Or most of them.

Conversely, if I rejected what was evident to me, if to no one else, then I would also be rejecting what I respected so greatly: that mankind's emancipation and upward struggle depends chiefly upon his translation of the unknown into the known, through the use of his intellect and the scientific principle.

That was the dilemma. It may have been truly the touch of a magic wand and a gift bestowed. I still don't know.

14.

THOUGHT-FORMS

Annie Besant and
Charles Webster Leadbeater

*Besant and Leadbeater investigated "thought-forms,"
the patterns of energy generated by an individual's emotions, quality of thought, and the body's metabolic processes.
The results of this detailed clairvoyant investigation is particularly striking, since the entire rhythms and properties of
the aura are seen as affected by the wide range of individual
thought that generated through it, and by the quality of
energy in the environment that these thoughts attract.*

* * *

What is called the aura of man is the outer part of the
cloudlike substance of his higher bodies, interpenetrating each other, and extending beyond the confines of his
physical body, the smallest of all. Two of these bodies, the
mental and desire bodies, are those chiefly concerned
with the appearance of what are called thought-forms.

Man, the thinker, is clothed in a body composed of
innumerable combinations of the subtle matter of the
mental plane, this body being more or less refined in its
constituents and organized more or less fully for its functions, according to the stage of intellectual development
at which the man himself has arrived. The mental body is
an object of great beauty, the delicacy and rapid motion
of its particles giving it an aspect of living iridescent light,
and this beauty becomes an extraordinarily radiant and
entrancing loveliness as the intellect becomes more
highly evolved and is employed chiefly on pure and sub-

lime topics. Every thought gives rise to a set of correlated vibrations in the matter of this body, accompanied with a marvellous play of color, like that in the spray of a water-fall as the sunlight strikes it, raised to the nth degree of color and vivid delicacy. The body under this impulse throws off a vibrating portion of itself, shaped by the nature of the vibrations—as figures are made by sand on a disk vibrating to a musical note—and this gathers from the surrounding atmosphere matter like itself in fineness from the elemental essence of the mental world. We have then a thought-form pure and simple, and it is a living entity of intense activity animated by the one idea that generated it. If made of the finer kinds of matter, it will be of great power and energy, and may be used as a most potent agent when directed by a strong and steady will.

When the man's energy flows outward toward external objects of desire, or is occupied in passional and emo-tional activities, this energy works in a less subtle order of matter than the mental, in that of the astral world. What is called his desire-body is composed of this matter, and it forms the most prominent part of the aura in the unde-veloped man. Where the man is of a gross type, the desire-body is of the denser matter of the astral plane, and is dull in hue, browns and dirty greens and reds playing a great part in it. Through this will flash various characteristic colors, as his passions are excited. A man of a higher type has his desire-body composed of the finer qualities of astral matter, with the colors, rippling over and flashing through it, fine and clear in hue. While less delicate and less radiant than the mental body, it forms a beautiful object, and as selfishness is eliminated all the duller and heavier shades disappear.

The desire (or astral) body gives rise to a second class of entities, similar in their general constitution to the thought-forms already described, but limited to the astral plane, and generated by the mind under the dominion of the animal nature.

These are caused by the activity of the lower mind, throwing itself out through the astral body—the activity of kāma-manas in theosophical terminology, or the mind dominated by desire. Vibrations in the body of desire are in this case set up and under these this body throws off a vibrating portion of itself, shaped, as in the previous case, by the nature of the vibrations, and this attracts to itself some of the appropriate elemental essence of the astral world. Such a thought-form has for its body this elemental essence, and for its animating soul the desire or passion which threw it forth; according to the amount of mental energy combined with this desire or passion will be the force of the thought-form. These, like those belonging to the mental plane, are called artificial elementals, and they are by far the most common, as few thoughts of ordinary men and women are untinged with desire, passion, or emotion.

Each definite thought produces a double effect—a radiating vibration and a floating form. The thought itself appears first to clairvoyant sight as a vibration in the mental body, and this may be either simple or complex. If the thought itself is absolutely simple, there is only the one rate of vibration, and only one type of mental matter will be strongly affected. The mental body is composed of matter of several degrees of density, which we commonly arrange in classes according to the sub-planes. Of each of these we have many sub-divisions, and if we typify these by drawing horizontal lines to indicate the different degrees of density, there is another arrangement which we might symbolize by drawing perpendicular lines at right angles to the others, to denote types which differ in quality as well as in density. There are thus many varieties of this mental matter, and it is found that each one of these has its own especial and appropriate rate of vibration, to which it seems most accustomed, so that it very readily responds to it, and tends to return to it as soon as possible when it has been forced away from it by some strong rush of thought or feeling. When a sudden wave of some emotion sweeps over a man, for example, his astral body is thrown into violent agitation, and its original colors are for the time almost obscured by the flush of carmine, of blue, or of scarlet which corresponds with the rate of vibration of that particular emotion. This change is only temporary; it passes off in a few seconds, and the astral body rapidly resumes its usual condition. Yet every such rush of feeling produces a permanent effect: it always adds a little of its hue to the normal coloring of the astral body, so that every time that the man yields himself to a certain emotion it becomes easier for him to yield himself to it again, because his astral body is getting into the habit of vibrating at that especial rate.

The majority of human thoughts, however, are by no means simple. Absolutely pure affection of course exists; but we very often find it tinged with pride or with selfishness, with jealousy or with animal passion. This means that at least two separate vibrations appear both in the mental and astral bodies—frequently more than two. The radiating vibration, therefore, will be a complex one, and the resultant thought-form will show several colors instead of only one.

These radiating vibrations, like all others in nature, become less powerful in proportion to the distance from their source, though it is probable that the variation is in proportion to the cube of the distance instead of to the square, because of the additional dimension involved. Again, like all other vibrations, these tend to reproduce themselves whenever opportunity is offered to them; and so whenever they strike upon another mental body they tend to provoke in it their own rate of motion. That is—from the point of view of the man whose mental body is touched by these waves—they tend to produce in his mind thoughts of the same type as that which had previously arisen in the mind of the thinker who sent forth the waves. The distance to which such thought-waves penetrate, and the force and persistency with which they impinge upon the mental bodies of others, depend upon the strength and clearness of the original thought. In this way the thinker is in the same position as the speaker. The voice of the latter sets in motion waves of sound in the air which radiate from him in all directions, and convey his message to all those who are within hearing, and the distance to which his voice can penetrate depends upon its power and upon the clearness of his enunciation. In just the same way the forceful thought will carry very much farther than the weak and undecided thought; but clearness and definiteness are of even greater importance than strength. Again, just as the speaker's voice may fall upon heedless ears where men are already engaged in business or in pleasure, so may a mighty wave of thought sweep past without affecting the mind of the man, if he be already deeply engrossed in some other line of thought.

It should be understood that this radiating vibration conveys the character of the thought, but not its subject. If a Hindu sits rapt in devotion to Krishna, the waves of feeling which pour forth from him stimulate devotional feeling in all those who come under their influence, though in the case of the Muhammadan that devotion is to Allah, while for the Zoroastrian it is to Ahuramazda, or for the Christian to Jesus. A man thinking keenly upon some high subject pours out from himself vibrations which tend to stir up thought at a similar level in others, but they in no way suggest to those others the special subject of his thought. They naturally act with special vigor upon those minds already habituated to vibrations of similar character; yet they have some effect on every mental body upon which they impinge, so that their tendency is to awaken the power of higher thought in those to whom it has not yet become a custom. It is thus evident that every man who thinks along high lines is doing missionary work, even though he may be entirely unconscious of it.

Let us turn now to the second effect of thought, the creation of a definite form. Students of the occult are acquainted with the idea of the elemental essence, that strange half-intelligent life which surrounds us in all directions, vivifying the matter of the mental and astral planes. This matter thus animated responds very readily to the influence of human thought, and every impulse sent out, either from the mental body or from the astral body of man, immediately clothes itself in a temporary vehicle of this vitalized matter. Such a thought or impulse becomes for the time a kind of living creature, the thought-force being the soul, and the vivified matter the body. Instead of using the somewhat clumsy paraphrase, "astral or mental matter ensouled by the monadic essence at the stage of one of the elemental kingdoms," theosophical writers often, for brevity's sake, call this quickened matter simply elemental essence; and sometimes they speak of the thought-form as "an elemental." There may be infinite variety in the color and shape of such elementals or thought-forms, for each thought draws round it the matter which is appropriate for its expression, and sets that matter into vibration in harmony with its own; so that the character of the thought decides its color, and the study of its variations and combinations is an exceedingly interesting one.

If the man's thought or feeling is directly connected with someone else, the resultant thought-form moves towards that person and discharges itself upon his astral and mental bodies. If the man's thought is about himself, or is based upon a personal feeling, as the vast majority of thoughts are, it hovers round its creator and is always ready to react upon him whenever he is for a moment in a passive condition. For example, a man who yields himself to thoughts of impurity may forget all about them while he is engaged in the daily routine of his business, even though the resultant forms are hanging round him in a heavy cloud, because his attention is otherwise directed and his astral body is therefore not impressible by any other rate of vibration than its own. When, however, the marked vibration slackens and the man rests after his labors and leaves his mind blank as regards definite thought, he is very likely to feel the vibration of impurity stealing insidiously upon him. If the consciousness of the man be to any extent awakened, he may perceive this and cry out that he is being tempted by the devil; yet the truth is that the temptation is from without only in appearance, since it is nothing but the natural reaction upon him of his own thought-forms. Each man travels through space enclosed within a case of his own building, surrounded by a mass of the forms created by his habitual thoughts. Through this medium he looks out upon the world, and naturally he sees everything tinged with its predominant colors, and all rates of vibration which reach him from without are more or less modified by its rate. Thus until the man learns complete control of thought and feeling, he sees nothing as it really is, since all his observations must be made through this medium, which distorts and colors everything like badly made glass.

If the thought-form be neither definitely personal nor specially aimed at someone else, it simply floats detached in the atmosphere, all the time radiating vibrations similar to those originally sent forth by its creator. If it does not come into contact with any other mental body, this radiation gradually exhausts its store of energy, and in that case the form falls to pieces; but if it succeeds in awakening sympathetic vibration in any mental body near at hand, an attraction is set up, and the thought-form is usually absorbed by that mental body. Thus we see that the influence of the thought-form is by no means so far-reaching as that of the original vibration; but insofar as it acts, it acts with much greater precision. What it produces in the mind-body which is influences is not merely a thought of an order similar to that which gave it birth; it is actually the same thought. The radiation may affect thousands and stir up in them thoughts on the same level as the original, and yet it may happen that no one of them will be identical with that original; the thought-form can affect only very few, but in those few cases it will reproduce exactly the initiatory idea.

From the point of view of the forms which they produce we may group thought into three classes:

1. That which takes the image of the thinker. When a man thinks of himself as in some distant place, or wishes earnestly to be in that place, he makes a thought-form in his own image which appears there. Such a form has not

infrequently been seen by others, and has sometimes been taken for the astral body or apparition of the man himself. In such a case, either the seer must have enough of clairvoyance for the time to be able to observe that astral shape, or the thought-form must have sufficient strength to materialize itself—that is, to draw round itself temporarily a certain amount of physical matter. The thought which generates such a form as this must necessarily be a strong one, and it therefore employs a larger proportion of the matter of the mental body, so that though the form is small and compressed when it leaves the thinker, it draws round it a considerable amount of astral matter, and usually expands to life-size before it appears at its destination.

2. That which takes the image of some material object. When a man thinks of his friend he forms within his mental body a minute image of that friend, which often passes outward and usually floats suspended in the air before him. In the same way if he thinks of a room, a house, a landscape, tiny images of these things are formed within the mental body and afterwards externalized. This is equally true when he is exercising his imagination; the painter who forms a conception of his future picture builds it up out of the matter of his mental body, and then projects it into space in front of him, keeps it before his mind's eye, and copies it. The novelist in the same way builds images of his character in mental matter, and by the exercise of his will moves these puppets from one position or grouping to another, so that the plot of his story is literally acted out before him. With our curiously inverted conceptions of reality it is hard for us to understand that these mental images actually exist, and are so entirely objective that they may readily be seen by the clairvoyant, and can even be rearranged by someone other than their creator. Some novelists have been dimly aware of such a process, and have testified that their characters when once created developed a will of their own, and insisted on carrying the plot of the story along lines quite different from those originally intended

by the author. This has actually happened, sometimes because the thought-forms were ensouled by playful nature-spirits, or more often because some "dead" novelist, watching on the astral plane the development of the plan of his fellow-author, thought that he could improve upon it, and chose this method of putting forward his suggestions.

3. That which takes a form entirely its own, expressing its inherent qualities in the matter which it draws round it. Only thought-forms of this third class can usefully be illustrated, for to represent those of the first or second class would be merely to draw portraits or landscapes. In those types we have the plastic mental or astral matter molded in imitation of forms belonging to the physical plane; in this third group we have a glimpse of the forms natural to the astral or mental planes. Yet this very fact, which makes them so interesting, places an insuperable barrier in the way of their accurate reproduction.

Thought-forms of this third class almost invariably manifest themselves upon the astral plane, as the vast majority of them are expressions of feeling as well as of thought. Those of which we here give specimens are almost wholly of that class, except that we take a few examples of the beautiful thought-forms created in definite meditation by those who, through long practice, have learnt how to think.

Thought-forms directed towards individuals produce definitely marked effects, these effects being either partially reproduced in the aura of the recipient and so increasing the total result, or repelled from it. A thought of love and of desire to protect, directed strongly towards some beloved object, creates a form which goes to the person thought of, and remains in his aura as a shielding and protecting agent; it will seek all opportunities to serve, and all opportunities to defend, not by a conscious and deliberate action, but by a blind following out of the impulse impressed upon it, and it will strengthen friendly forces that impinge on the aura and weaken unfriendly ones. Thus may we create and maintain veritable guardian angels round those we love, and many a mother's prayer for a distant child thus circles round him, though she knows not the method by which her "prayer is answered."

In cases in which good or evil thoughts are projected at individuals, those thoughts, if they are to fulfil directly their mission, must find, in the aura of the object to whom they are sent, materials capable of responding sympathetically to their vibrations. Any combination of matter can only vibrate within certain definite limits, and if the thought-form be outside all the limits within which the aura is capable of vibrating, it cannot affect that aura at all. It consequently rebounds from it, and that with a force proportionate to the energy with which it impinged upon it. This is why it is said that a pure heart and mind are the best protectors against any inimical assaults, for such a pure heart and mind will construct an astral and a mental body of fine and subtle materials, and these bodies cannot respond to vibrations that demand coarse and dense matter. If an evil thought, projected with malefic intent, strikes such a body, it can only rebound from it, and it is flung back with all its own energy; it then flies backward along the magnetic line of least resistance, that which it has just traversed, and strikes its projector; he, having matter in his astral and mental bodies similar to that of the thought-form he generated, is thrown into respondent vibrations, and suffers the destructive effects he had intended to cause to another. Thus "curses (and blessings) come home to roost." So long as any of the coarser kinds of matter connected with evil and selfish thoughts remain in a person's body, he is open to attack from those who wish him evil, but when he has perfectly eliminated these by self-purification his haters cannot injure him, and he goes on calmly and peacefully amid all the darts of their malice. But it is bad for those who shoot out such darts.

15

AURA AND THE SEANCE

Phoebe D. Payne and
Laurence J. Bendit

In this selection by psychiatrist Laurence J. Bendit and Phoebe D. Payne, a clairvoyant, the idea that energy can be transferred from one person to another via the aura is examined in the context of a spiritualistic circle or séance.

In light of the recent explosion of interest in possession, Bendit and Payne offer a significant and plausible explanation of how an individual may be overwhelmed by thoughts from others. This is especially apparent when this selection is read in conjunction with Besant and Leadbeater's "Thought-Forms."

* * *

Whether we are considering a private sitting of one or two people with a medium, or a circle consisting of a greater number, the psychic mechanics are very much the same, and, if we are to understand them they need to be looked at in terms of group psychology. As we have already said, we cannot, from a scientific angle, be certain whether the psyche is pure abstraction, or whether it is a quasi-material object with a shape and structure which can be expressed in physical terms. In any case, to the clairvoyant it presents itself as such an object, and whether we consider this to be merely symbolic or whether it is really an object is a theoretical point. The objective view is the more convenient, and gives us the easiest—if not in an absolute sense the truest—way of discussing its behaviour.

Most clairvoyants tell us that they see each person surrounded by a luminous cloud or aura, extending usually some two or three feet beyond the confines of the body. This is analogous to an electro-magnetic field, but does not register on the most sensitive physical instruments yet devised because the energy it represents is mental and emotional, not physical. Maybe it represents a higher octave of energy waves, but it is certainly something different from the range covered by phenomena known in the physical world.

This human aura has long been the subject of much discussion among psychics, and, although a lot has been written about it, in the last analysis very little is actually known. At first sight it appears to the trained clairvoyant as an oval cloud of swiftly moving multi-coloured mist. It surrounds the dense physical body and extends beyond it in all directions. It is not confined to a special shape, but is always shifting and changing as the thought and feeling of its owner changes. The quality, colours and tone-range of this aura are determined by the nature of the thought and feeling with which they are connected, so that the aura is intensely personal. It is so responsive, both to inner and outer stimuli, that it is seldom quiescent, and is always re-acting to its environment. This is an important fact to note, especially in dealing with the composite group aura which is formed between two or more persons in close proximity.

Each person enters the séance room with his psychic field or aura intact, and shaped around his own body. But when he has been sitting for some time near another, and in a receptive frame of mind, his own aura tends to lose its definite outline and to become merged into the aura of his neighbour. In this way a number of persons together, after a time, share a common aura. It is as though someone brought into the room a number of cups of liquid on a tray, then gradually emptied each cup into the tray itself.

This group aura has as its greatest common measure the united qualities of thought and feeling emanating from the members of the group. Thus, an unrecognised telepathic rapport is set up, and feeling flows across this group aura without distinction as to the source from which it emerges. It is almost as though the group became enclosed in a fine film of ultra-responsive material, and through this film every faintest ripple in the atmosphere recorded itself. The medium is, generally speaking, very sensitive to this condition, and is often aware in two directions. In one direction, there is an increased perception of the inner world, so that details of thought and feeling become much clearer. To this is added a greatly enhanced range of knowledge, which is generally accredited to a guide or the person out of the body, who is said to be in communication with a member of the group. There is also a strange penetration into the sitters' thoughts and emotions, so that they lie open to the medium in a way that does not happen unless both medium and sitter are enclosed within one aura.

It sometimes happens that a sitter is more sensitive to the group aura than the medium, and is baffled and surprised by the amount of knowledge and perception that seems to flow into her from nowhere in particular. This is well-known to people who frequent the séance room. They will often say, after the group, that they knew what was coming before it found any expression, and that they were personally aware of every description or message that the medium gave.

At other times one special person willy-nilly dominates the whole proceedings. The medium is unable to do other than pick out information for that one person. Even when the sitter concerned becomes apologetic and embarrassed by the amount of attention thus aroused, the current still continues to flow in his direction. In point of fact this means that that individual has strong thoughts or desires which make a clear and definite impression on the group aura and, through it, upon the sensitive field of the medium's mind. Any person of dominant thought and feeling, whether these be conscious or unconscious is apt to throw out clear images and ideas which are much more sharply recorded on the composite aura than those of the muddled thinker, or an emotionally confused person who makes a faint impression on it. It is as if the medium were in a room full of pictures, some of which are bright and sharp, others vague and dull. His attention will naturally be drawn to those which strike him most vividly.

The group aura becomes as it were an entity in the psychic world. But although thought and emotion tend to become pooled in the way we have described, it is only a relative and temporary fusion. It is as if the individual aura lost its periphery, so that its contents melted into its neighbours, but the central core of that aura, the psychological ego, remained. Thus at the end of the séance, when the circle breaks up, each ego gathers round itself once more the material which it has put into the pool. It is as if one imagined a collection of one-celled amoebae coming together and coalescing so that for the time being one had a large protoplasmic mass in which the nucleus of each amoeba was embedded. At the end of the séance, each amoeba draws its protoplasm back to itself, encloses it in the rather vague film which is the cell-wall, and departs on its own business. The person with a clear-cut positive mind reintegrates himself with his own material, and that only. But the suggestible person can pick up material from other people as well as his own, and so can go away more or less influenced by this additional material, somewhat as a sponge absorbs water. This is due to a negative attitude of mind. There are many such people frequenting public circles and smaller séances, and in course of time they can find themselves in difficulties and may get into deep waters, because they do not realise what is happening to them. This type of person is in need of psychological help because it does not occur to him to stop negative psychic practices, even if those practices are very simple and only consist of attendance at a circle. Failing that, they may go from bad to worse, gradually becoming more confused and anxious because their own thoughts and feelings have become confused with others by psychic contamination. This can even influence physical health, and the person may become one of the baffling type of patient, whom every doctor knows to be genuinely ill, but for whose illness he can find no valid physical reason. Common symptoms, in bad cases, are constant hearing of voices, repetitions of visions and obsessional thoughts, none of which can be shut out. Unfortunately, the unimaginative physician, in such cases, has no better idea of treatment than to give his patient the universal panacea of to-day, phenobarbitone. This, though it may to some extent mask the insomnia and the anxiety, is, by the very nature of the patient's negative condition, likely to cause further and deeper deterioration. Some doctors are wise enough to send this sort of patient to a psychologist, and he in his turn is likely to be frustrated because he may trace the immediate cause of the trouble to attending séances, and equally rightly may discover that the deeper root comes from earlier predisposition, but he is not in a position to perceive or assess the amount of psychic contagion which has taken place. The difficulty is that so often the sufferer cannot get right until he has cleared his aura of the extraneous material. These patients often have the idea that they are possessed by a discarnate spirit. This is not so at all, but the obsession is real insofar as they have allowed thought-material from other people to trespass into their own personal field. The cure, in general terms, lies in discontinuing all negative psychic practices such as sittings, automatic writing, planchette, or even fortune-telling for amusement, as well as in trying to find a positive psychological integration.

The fact that slight remnants of differentiation persist in the circle after it has "grouped" is one of the reasons why a medium will often ask friendly and emotionally warm people to sit next to her, rather than the intellectuals. For when she is under any degree of trance, her waking consciousness loses its defences, and makes her much more vulnerable to mass impacts from the conglomerate aura around her. For instance, an impatient thought of criticism from a sitter, if directed straight to the medium, will act exactly like a sharp instrument striking her. It can produce real shock and pain. On the other hand, criticism alone will not be detrimental, provided it is not used destructively and with an emotional drive propelling it. Very few people realise that a hypersensitive medium is often hurt more by the emotion behind a thought than by the thought itself.

Like any other psychological group, the aura in a circle represents the aggregation of the minds of those present. The unconscious as well as the conscious minds of the sitters play into it, so that the *quality* of the aura is determined by all those present, as well as by their common motive in coming together. Returning to the analogy of the cups of liquid, it is as if one were to pour cups of salt water of varying strength into the tray. The result would be a solution of strength proportionate to the amount of strong, medium, or weak solution poured in. Consequently also, the nature of the group will depend on the kinds of chemicals which are put it. Some of them will combine and mix happily, whereas others will tend to effervesce, or to become hot and explosive. Others may refuse altogether to mix, and hence, as the experienced sitter knows, the circle does not function at all.

Once more, however, physical analogies are not perfect because the aura of the group is highly labile and suggestible—that is, sensitive to every change of atmosphere. As has been pointed out, the common purpose in coming together is an important factor. Therefore, a group of sober students is more likely to produce worth-while material, than another of frivolous or highly emotional and uncritical folk who are only anxious to be reassured and comforted. These will form a circle of quite a different nature. Any group aura is highly influenced by strong thought among its members, and not only by outside influences which may come into it. This idea is not likely to appeal to those who wish to believe that there is an inner spiritual guidance at the back of it. This was proved by one of the writers (P.D.P.) who, to the dismay of some of the intelligent members of her circle, used to predict what would happen during the evening's work. She discovered that while sitting with an experimental circle of twelve to fifteen people, whose purpose was to try to help the medium to develop "direct voice" phenomena, that is, an attempt to reproduce the actual voice of the communicator, a thing far more difficult than the usual method of communication, which takes place in the medium's own intonation.

The group itself was an interesting one. It consisted of engineers, civil servants, an architect, a doctor, and professional men and women. They were a purely experimental group, and interested in the rationale and mechanics of psychism. The writer accidentally discovered that, when she got tired of the uninteresting generalities of the medium, she could make something happen by thinking it. She would for instance focus on one member of the group and imagine some special incident connected with that person, such as the death of an elderly man of a particular appearance. Almost immediately a message or description would be given that was a duplicate of the thought she had constructed. She pointed this fact out tentatively first to an engineer, and later to other members of the group. They discussed the matter and tried simple experiments, which confirmed that the communication could be influenced in one direction or another. It was like tilting a table, or swinging a compass in any given direction. The medium was entirely ignorant that this discussion had arisen, and the other members of the group were, at first, quite sceptical about the whole thing. But one evening before the group met, this investigator told the engineer there would be a visit that evening from the entirely fictitious fiancée he had never possessed. Surely enough, during the evening, the man was addressed through or by the medium, by a young woman, telling him she was with him in death as in life, that she still loved him and was guiding and looking after him from the spirit world—in short, all the usual things which one might expect in such a case. Gradually, it became clear, in that group at any rate, that a strongly projected thought produced commensurate results. It was all very dismaying, because no one had any clue to the problem, and no one, at that time, possessed any psychological knowledge. It was such a blow to the group that they decided to abandon the experiments.

Needless to say, this was not done out of malice or mischief, nor with the slightest ill-feeling towards the medium, but in the spirit of investigation, which was the alleged purpose of the organisation which ran the circle. But—and unfortunately experienced investigators will know this is only too common—when the head of the organisation was told about the experiments, instead of accepting them in a scientific spirit, he was very angry. To be unwilling to face facts of this order is one of the reasons for the continuing confusion among *bona fide* spiritualists.

One more factor needs to be taken into account, in spiritualistic circles as in other groups—and here again the analogy of the cups of water is incomplete. For, when we are dealing with living organisms, the result of integration into a greater group is not merely a sum of the parts. It is something more, as if the group itself acquired a temporary nuclear ego round which it focused and revolved, as planets do round the sun.

This focus must, in the nature of things, be connected with the purpose of the group. Where people meet together to try and make contact with the so-called dead, the focus will, from the point of view of the living, go half-way towards making that contact possible, provided they do not ruin everything by being more interested in themselves than in the actual dead person. So that, assuming the dead can and want to communicate with the living, they, too, have to do only half the work required to build the bridge which makes such communication possible. From the point of view of the dead, therefore, one can postulate that the sensitive group aura may be a valuable and easy instrument or magnetic field for them to influence. For, if they themselves are living, bodiless, yet with their psychological equipment intact, the field of the circle, belonging as it does to the same level of the universe as that where they are themselves living, is obviously suitable for them to influence from their side.

16

THE BRITTLE AURA

Society of Rosicrucians

How can we protect ourselves from the influence of others? How does fear prevent spiritual development? This selection may be viewed, in part, as a brief summary of occult wisdom through the ages.

* * *

Man in his ignorance, believes he has control of himself by placing a hard exterior, first to his body, then to his mind, by appearing immovable, and third, to his soul by seeming and appearing to be unemotional and protected by a brittle aura. He then feels pride; he is in full command of himself. Nothing can reach him! Nothing can touch him! Yes—he is right,—nothing *can* touch him, nothing *can* reach him. *He is a slave to himself. He is imprisoned within himself and knows it not.* He is a sad spectacle and is ignorant of the fact.

Just as the skin on the physical body is an outer covering or casing, containing the physical organs, etc., of the body, and protecting them from outer frictions, so the aura, in its own way, *is the skin or outer covering of the astral body.* Probably you have never thought of it in this light. The human aura is, to a large extent, the key to the soul, for through that aura one reaches or rather, reads the soul of another.

Man's protective instinct is caused and developed through *fear*—fear of the *unknown*. The same applies to the aura. Emotional fear will cause a brittle aura. The aura is normally hardened, like the skin, but a brittle aura is one that is fragile, easily broken or wrenched apart, leaving openings through which other influences can reach in or penetrate. Normally, the aura is hardened as a protector. Protector of what, you ask? A self-created protector that is the opposite to the brittleness that we bring about by opening ourselves to fear and all its synonyms.

A brittle aura is the greatest obstacle to spiritual growth. Those having brittle auras not only have to help themselves from *within*, but strangely, they have to be helped from without as well. They have locked themselves within, but part of the key is without.

A strange paradox, you say?

Think it over!

When your physical skin *is very dry it becomes brittle*; it cracks easily and you bleed from within and friction from without is painful for it causes further cracking or splitting of the skin. We are referring to diseased skin or skin infections. You correct this condition both internally and externally through proper regulation of diet, medical aid and the application of soothing, healing oils or salves to the outer skin. The same law applies to the aura. The inner healing comes from *within*; the outer from our environment and outer experiences. But the real healing is always from *within*; the outer is only a help, not a *cure*.

Man, at present, is in the process of building three vehicles at the same time. The most perfected so far, is his physical structure. His astral body is far from perfect and far from under control. His so-called mental body is only a sheath not yet a body, and is therefore, the most imperfect.

The human aura is not only akin to the physical covering or skin of man in its functions to the astral body, but far more than that. The human aura is the radiation or emanation of electronic energy as contained in each vehicle. This radiation or emanation is either in control of the astral or it is not. Either it controls the astral or it is controlled by the astral body, according to individual development. The human aura is both physical and spiritual, just as electricity is both physical and spiritual.

The human aura not only indicates the *vitality of the body*, but the vitality of the soul as well. It is an emanation of a radio-active nature and envelops all of man's vehicles. The human aura, therefore, can be called man's *spiritual skin*, for it is sensitive to both inner and outer impacts. It can be translucent, opaque, thick, heavy, light, radiant, thin as tissue and impenetrable as the strongest steel at the same time. It can be porous as a sponge, brittle as glass, and soggy as mud. In colors, there is no limit to what it can produce by way of variations. For color is vibration and the aura *feeds* on vibration and *produces* vibration. Another paradox!

Just as your physical skin both *protects* and *receives*, so the human aura *protects* and *receives* likewise. Both sympathy and antipathy are sensed through the aura. Personal magnetism and the human aura are close companions. As control over our vehicles increases, personal magnetism has greater facility for expression and the human aura increases its power of extension and influence.

You feel the influence of a person through the aura. Our Great Master, the Christ, had an aura that extended tremendously and could be sensed *for miles*. It now envelops the entire planet.

The aura is, in reality, the *radiance of the soul*. Many labor in the fear of obsession and all that it implies. *Fear itself*, is the *easiest channel* for an obsessing entity to use.

Remember that love and fear cannot exist together. Love is the *greatest power* there is. He who truly radiates love, not sentimentality or its many equivalents, but true, whole-hearted love, *fears nothing*.

The brittle aura is becoming more and more common because of the increase of fear, doubt, confusion, greed and the many human failings that man is indulging in at the present time. . . .

The person with a healthy, normal aura finds it possible to associate with *all* types of persons. He who can associate only with a limited group has the answer in his aura. Many, who have studied the human aura, pride themselves on their ability of being *so sensitive* that they can associate only with those who are in complete harmony with themselves. The truly evolved soul *is in control* and is not *controlled*. That is why our Great Master was able to associate with those who had disorganized auras and brought order and love into their lives.

The brittle aura is the product of fear, doubt, uncertainty, greed, jealousy, envy, etc. Every time anyone indulges in these, the aura becomes brittle, fragile, and, as a result, fractures, leaving gaps here and there, and these points or places of least resistance are opened for many things. If these negative qualities are indulged in constantly and frequently, it becomes more and more difficult to soften the aura, and its natural state becomes so crystallized that it is permanently brittle. Then you deal with a truly *self-imprisoned soul*.

You ask, "How can you help such a condition?" The answer is so simple that it is one of the most difficult to do—LOVE. Love has many by-paths. It has kindliness, sympathy, and real understanding, consideration, patience and thoughtfulness.

Take the most brittle aura and apply these qualities from *without* and stimulate the intent and purpose to change from *within* and your brittle aura will soon become soft, pliable and *strong*.

The human aura is an *index* to your soul.

17.

THE SCIENTIFIC STUDY
OF
THE HUMAN AURA

Charles T. Tart

Charles T. Tart is a psychology professor at the Univer-
sity of California at Davis, whose main interest has been in
altered states of consciousness and psi experience.
Tart takes a much-needed critical and close look at the
kinds of scientific problems that arise in researching the
aura and offers methods to test for its existence.

* * *

I am going to discuss primarily the methodological problems of trying to study the human aura. I shall not try to
review the literature about the aura, but take a basic
position that although there is a lot of nonsense in this
area, there may be some genuine, important phenomena. Given that, how do we begin to collect some hard
data about this problem? How do we get *reliable* and *valid*
types of observation that can enable us to understand
what the aura is, how we might use it, and so on? I am
going to define the aura in a very minimal way as simply a
something that is perceived by human beings, and is perceived as a something that surrounds a person. We will
call that latter person the target person.

Figure 1 shows an observer who sees this aura surrounding the target person. Thus the aura is minimally

defined as a something, associated with the space immediately surrounding a target person that an observer can see.

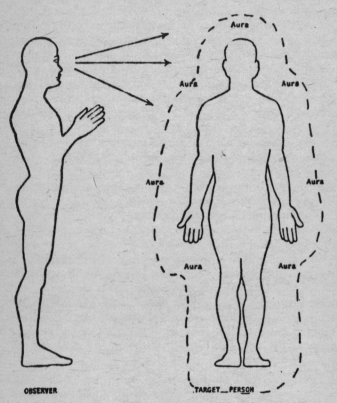

FIG. 1. The Basic Situation in Observation of the Human Aura.

Confounding of Physical and Aural Information

To begin with, in talking about the target person's aura we have to remember that in practically all cases we hear of not only is the observer presumably looking at the target person's aura, he is also looking at the target person. The physical appearance of the target person comprises a large body of information. You can see a great deal about people simply by looking at them, their posture, the way they move, the way they dress, the way they groom themselves, etc. This leads to a great confounding when someone gives an aura reading because you do not know how much of the information that is being produced is information that actually exists in some sense "in" the target person's aura, and how much comes from physically observable characteristics of the target person, whether static characteristics or behaviour. At one extreme, for instance, an observer ostensibly doing an aura reading may say a number of valid things about the target person, but they may have nothing to do with any such thing as an aura. They are characteristics that a good observer of human beings can pick up from their outward physical characteristics.

The first methodological problem that has to be dealt with then, is, how do you separate out these two sources of information so that you know when you are dealing with the aura? The way that it *should* be done, and which has practically never been done in the research that I know of, is that all sensorily perceivable information from the target person himself must be blocked. So there is no *sensory* information to pick up, and the only information available is in the hypothetical aura. How do you do this?

The Doorway Test

I developed an appropriate test many years ago, which I have never had a chance to apply for lack of good aura readers. I call it the "doorway test." First: to optimize conditions, you let your sensitive find a target person who has a *big* aura, one that sticks out a lot and is stable over time. It is not something that fades out every couple of minutes, or something like that, it is a steady, big surround.

Second: you then block the target person's physical characteristics by the simple expedient of having the target person stand behind the edge of a doorway. His shoulders should be just behind it, so that none of his physical body is visible to the sensitive, *but his aura sticks out several inches beyond the doorway*. The basic setup is shown in aerial view in Figure 2. More elaborate shields could be used, but doorways are generally available.

Third: you set up a random trial schedule, where sometimes the target person does stand *immediately* behind the doorway, sometimes he stands ten feet farther back from the doorway. On each of these trials an experimenter, who is with the sensitive, asks: "Is the aura protruding beyond the doorway or not?"

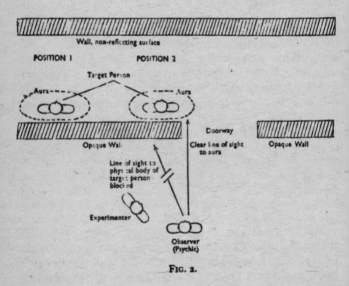

FIG. 2.

If the sensitive is objectively perceiving the aura, there should be practically one hundred percent success in saying that either the person is right by the doorway or that the person is *not* right by the doorway.

This is a simple, straightforward test in theory. In

practice you have to eliminate all sensory cues, such as reflecting surfaces. You can't use noisy target people who clump their way back and forth to the doorway. The experimenter with the sensitive should not know where the target person is on any given trial, etc. But it is relatively easy at present to eliminate these sorts of cue.

This test will deal with the first methodological problem, separating out the target person's *physical* characteristics from information that might be "located" in this aura that surrounds the target person. What I am saying, in another way, is that we have to be careful not to ascribe to the *aura* characteristics which are picked up from sensory observation of the target person himself.

The Physical Aura

The next point I want to make is that we have to distinguish between several distinct types of aura, and make it clear which one we are trying to study at any given time, which one we are talking about. Otherwise we are going to get into a lot of confusion. The first kind of aura is what I shall call the *physical aura*. By "physical," I mean physical in the ordinary sense of the word, matter or energy fields that immediately surround the target person. This means that, in principle, the physical aura should be detectable by known physical instruments.

Now we know that there *is* a physical aura. For instance, a person is sweating: this means that there are a variety of organic molecules mixed with water vapour in the immediate vicinity of his body. A person is usually warm with respect to his surroundings, so there are thermal gradients and resultant air currents in the air immediately around him. Thermal (infrared) energy is being radiated from the body. There is an electrostatic field around a person, and electrical ion fields (ionized particles and gases) surround him. Electromagnetic radiation (radio waves) in the microwave region of the spectrum is emitted at a low level, as well as low frequency electromagnetic radiation of up to one hundred kilocycles being generated by muscle action and possibly radiated. At any given time, any or all of these possible "auras" may exist in a complex mixture around a person's body.

Now, one of the first research questions that we have to deal with is: is this physical aura actually detectable either by instruments or human observers? It is quite possible that while *in principle* this physical aura exists, in practice it exists at such a weak level of intensity that you cannot detect it; that atmospheric noise is so great that you cannot really detect the physical aura.

In practice, instruments can detect some things around the human body. For instance if you have a sensitive water vapour detector and put it up close to the human body you will get a reading on this, because atmospheric water molecules will tend to be denser immediately in the vicinity of the skin. Electrostatic fields, electrical ion clouds, thermal radiation, (exceptionally weak) magnetic fields, and microwave radiation have been detected around humans under special circumstances. The important question with respect to the physical aura, however, is whether observers can detect the physical aura. Are human beings' known sensory mechanisms sensitive enough, under *any* kinds of condition, actually to detect the physical aura? Could a person for instance, see the air turbulence around another person rising from the thermal radiation? By and large, we would say no, or find only trivial cases: we are not amazed that a human can sense the warmth of another's body a few inches away. But suppose a sensitive passed the doorway test, reliably indicated whether the target person was close to the doorway edge or not? Would this indicate that the physical aura was detectable by known human senses, such as vision?

Unfortunately, the interpretation is not quite so simple, because you also have the possibility of *clairvoyant* detection, or detection of the physical aura by extrasensory means. While we have an immense amount of evidence for the reality of something like clairvoyance, we have little information on what the *limits* of this kind of faculty are. No one could authoritatively say, for instance, that you could *not* detect an ionic cloud around a person by using clairvoyance, even though you may be able to put up a good argument on theoretical grounds, or show practically, that the *known* human senses are not sensitive enough to pick up this aspect of the physical aura.

Another research problem with the physical aura is whether the characteristics of the physical aura show a variation over time, or are a permanent structure that correlates only with the long-term characteristics of the target person. At one extreme, the physical aura might be a rather static phenomenon—it is there if you are alive and gone if you are dead, and that is about the maximum amount of information you can get from it. On the other hand, there may be variations in these various components of the physical aura which would relate to changes in physiological activity, mental activity, etc. If this were so, they might be of interest not only in and of themselves, they might provide practically useful information. There might be an advantage in observing the physical aura of a person through appropriate instrumental or clairvoyant means in order to tell something about the person.

Or there might not be. This is an empirical question. For instance, you might devise a hundred thousand dollar instrument that could measure a person's body temperature by focusing on his aura alone. But why should you do that when a clinical thermometer would do the trick for you? So the question of the *usefulness* of the kind of information you can pick up from the physical aura is an empirical question that we simply have to work out.

With respect to the possible correlation of physical aura characteristics with the target person's internal state, another interesting research question arises: can a person learn volitional control over his physical aura? Can he learn to do things which will alter its characteristics, such as intensify it to make it more accessible for observation, or to perform better some of the functions that have been hypothesized for the aura? For instance, in some of the occult literature the aura is described as acting as a protective barrier to incoming stimuli. Somehow it protects a person from the shock of stimulus input. Might the physical (or other types of) aura perform such a function? I'm interested in this possibility because of my own research in the area of bio-feedback, where all sorts of biological and physiological processes that were formerly considered involuntary and totally beyond human control can now be brought under volitional control by giving people appropriate feedback signals through the right kinds of instruments.

Another important research question with respect to the physical aura is: how does the environment (both the physical and psychological environment) affect the physical aura? May it change its detectability, for instance? For example, from known physical principles we would predict that clothing would dissipate or disorganize the physical aura. You can't build up much of a layer of sweat-saturated air while leaving layers of cloth under your arms. What are the things that will shield the physical aura? Will atmospheric turbulence have major effects on this sort of aura? Is there any way of varying environmental conditions that will deliberately affect the physical aura? Increase its detectability? Kirlian photography, e.g., seems to be a way of environmentally affecting the physical aura.

Another important research question is: can the environmental conditions that an experimenter can alter deliberately change the correlation of the physical aura with physical and psychological characteristics of the person? That is, if we hypothesize the physical aura as depicting information about the internal state of the target person, might some environmental conditions wash out a particular correlation, so that the aura could no longer give you a valid reading of that particular information? These are all sorts of things that we need to know.

Now I have talked so far as if people were rather static and you could go in and examine them at any time. If there is one thing we do know about people from psychology, it is that a given person varies a great deal from time to time, and that when you look at more than one person there is a tremendous variability between persons. I cannot stress enough how important it is to begin to study the sources of variability between people, the dimensions of differences, and what causes these particular sorts of differences.

The physical aura would be detectable in this kind of doorway test that I talk about. If you can find some kind of physical emanation around a person that sticks out you should, with the proper instruments or a person whose sensory mechanisms are keen enough, be able to do extremely well in predicting when a person is right around the corner and when he is not.

The Psychological Aura

There is an entirely different type of aura that we can talk about, which I shall call the *psychological aura*, or the phenomenological aura. By this I mean that there is no physical or psychical "thing" of any sort that actually occupies the space around the person. Rather, the target person has a *mental concept* that "something" occupies the space immediately around him. That is, a psychological aura is a mental construct *concerning* the immediate space around the target person, and it exists only in the target person's mind. It has no existence independent of the target person's mental state.

This concept may be conscious, semi-conscious, or even unconscious. Many people act as if they possess a psychological aura, but if you ask them if they have an aura, is there something special in the space around them, they give you a blank look: what are you talking about? They do not sense it themselves, so clearly this sort of thing can exist on an unconscious level.

A typical reaction, in our culture, to the idea of a

psychological aura is to say that it is *subjective*. Subjective has quite negative connotations. Subjective means it is not real, you cannot study it, and it is unreliable. But that is not the case with the psychological aura: it is quite amenable to study, even though it does not have an existence independent of the target person's own conscious or unconscious concepts. You can study the psychological aura by observing a person's behaviour and/or by asking him about his feelings. From this data you can infer what his psychological aura is like.

For instance, consider the target person depicted in Figure I. At any given time, there are various sensory stimuli coming in to him which are affecting his experience and his behaviour. Added to these are various internal factors: his thought, his fantasies, his feelings, etc., which are also affecting his behaviour. These result in some external behaviour and some internal behaviour (inferred from his report of what he is experiencing). Our observer can observe these sorts of thing, and might say, from a long series of observations, "This person is acting *as if* he has a field 3 feet wide around him, and as if that field is bigger in the front than it is at the sides," or something like that.

I am not speaking hypothetically here, and I am going to illustrate in a minute actual research that has been carried out on the psychological aura.

For the sake of completeness, I want to note that the same sorts of problem can be thought about with respect to the psychological aura as to the physical aura. For instance, what about its detectability? What kinds of observation are best for inferring the psychological aura? What sorts of thing does a person do which are most revealing about his concept of the aura? What kinds of instruments would record a person's psychological aura? The correlations of the psychological aura with the person's own inner characteristics are again a fertile area for investigation. If you go to the trouble of observing these characteristics, and you infer a psychological aura from them as an explanation of the target person's behaviour, what will that tell you about other aspects of the person's behaviour?

Is it useful? Again, we have the possibility that we may develop an elaborate scheme for observing people under certain conditions inferring what their psychological aura is like, then trying to predict what they will do next. But you may get a very low level of predictability. So there is a real question here of acquiring useful measures in a practical sense.

As with the physical aura, we can look at the effect of environments on the detectability of the psychological aura, its correlates, etc. We can ask research questions about the function of the psychological aura. If a person has a psychological aura of such and such characteristics, *why* does he have it? What does it do for him? What does he gain from it? What does he lose from it? How does it affect his transactions with the world, etc.? How does it affect his personality, his self-concept, and various things like that?

We might also take up a related research question. How could you train the target person to sense his own psychological aura, and would this be a useful thing for him to do, to be aware of what this psychological construct is that he is carrying around with him, and of its effect on his behaviour?

Now let me illustrate that I am not just talking hypothetically at this point. A number of psychologists have done research on the psychological aura, although they have not done it under the name of aura research: after all, they're respectable people and to use a bad word like that. . . . They've done it under the concept of "personal space." It has been observed that people act *as if* there is something special about the space immediately around them, and that the space may be quite sharply defined.

A number of investigators have done what we might call *invasion* studies. They have mapped out a target person's personal space by invading it and seeing at what distance he moves away or reports feeling uncomfortable. One of my colleagues (Sommer, 1969) has done many invasions of personal space in libraries, e.g., he has an experimenter pick out target people who have been studying alone. The experimenter will then sit down at various distances from the target persons, and note how close he has to sit to get people to flee within various time limits.

You can study this another way by simply explaining the idea to a person, explaining that: "Sometimes when people get very close to you, you get uncomfortable. Okay, we want to map this sort of thing. You stand here, and I'm going to walk toward you very slowly, and tell me at what point you get uncomfortable." People have been found to have differently shaped personal spaces this way. A person's personal space is usually much bigger in front. It may stick out a foot, two feet, something like that. In general, you can get much closer in on the side before he gets uncomfortable, closer in on the back than you can on the front.

This kind of mapping can be affected by psychological effects. If you walk toward a person with a knife in your hand, I suspect his personal space will become somewhat larger! But allowing for these sorts of thing, you still find that for many people there's a stably defined area, immediately around them. They act as if it is a very special kind of area, and if people, except under very special circumstances, penetrate into that personal space, they generally become uncomfortable.

The size and shape of the psychological aura gotten by this mapping technique will vary with the type of invasion. It will vary with whether it is a person or a material object invading it. You can put a hatrack closer to a person without his feeling uncomfortable, in many instances, than you can another person. The janitor can come farther into your personal space than your boss. There are fairly stable differences among individuals here. This research is in its infancy.

There are considerable cultural differences: the personal space of South Europeans tends to be smaller than the personal space of Americans. One of the things that you frequently find at a cocktail party, shall we say, is a South European backing an American across a room. As the South European moves to the limit of his personal space, the American backs away, but the South European has not had his smaller personal space violated.

The uncomfortableness of invasion has been put to practical use. In some police interrogation manuals, they tell you that the interrogator should sit directly across from the suspect, with no table or anything in-between, and at first should sit a few feet away. But as the interrogation proceeds, the interrogator keeps moving in until he's just about touching the suspect. This will get the suspect nervous enough to be more likely to confess!

Another study I have carried out on the psychological aura is also quite interesting. Several years ago I began to wonder if you could take the personal space construct and not make it just an inferred thing, but teach people to "sense it" directly while hypnotized. I first began experimenting in some group situations, with untrained subjects who had various degrees of hypnotizability. Before hypnotizing the group, I would explain the psychological concept of personal space. After hypnotizing them, I would tell them: "All right, over the next minute or two something is going to happen, so you're going to *directly* experience this personal space around you. I don't know *exactly* how *you* will experience it. You might *see* it. You might *feel* it. You might *smell* it. You might do something I couldn't possibly conceive of, but in the next minute you're going to begin to sense your personal space." I've done this same sort of thing with well-trained hypnotic subjects in a more systematic manner also.

I found that most hypnotic subjects, even those who do not have a great deal of talent for hypnosis, who can only get into light to medium levels of hypnosis, will consciously detect their personal space after this procedure. Some of them will say they see something very dimly. Others will say there is something that feels "elastic" right around them, and they can tell when somebody bumps into it. They are bumping this tenuous elastic thing. Others will say it's a "vibration" feeling. Their eyes can be open, if they can still maintain hypnosis, without disturbing this "sensing" of the psychological aura.

Some people, once I've explained the idea of personal space, can begin to "sense" it without being hypnotized. Just to know that there is something they can look for is sufficient to let them "sense" this psychological aura.

Some other very interesting things can be done with the psychological aura under hypnosis. One of the things I did was to give subjects suggestions systematically to vary the size of their personal space. For instance, I would tell them their personal space was going to shrink until it did not extend beyond the boundaries of their skin. With practically every subject I have done this with, they report that this is a very unpleasant state. They feel pains, they feel unprotected, they get nervous, they feel off-balance. They don't like this kind of condition at all. On the other hand, I have also suggested that they expand their personal space to three times its original size. Almost all subjects report they really like this. It's euphoric, they feel cushioned, happy. If I tell them to expand it to the size of the whole room, most subjects report that when this happens their perception of it just fades out completely, and it's no longer there.

One of the interesting possibilities here is that while we talk about the psychological aura, a purely *inferential* construct, perhaps the person is not simply carrying around the mental construct, but actually detecting to some extent his own psychical aura or his physical aura.

Now, again, for investigating the psychological aura, I'd stress the importance of individual variability, which tends to be overlooked. I suspect there may be very different types of people with respect to the personal space they have.

The Psychical Aura

Now let us turn to a third type of aura, which I will call

the *psychical aura*, to use the old-fashioned term. By this I mean a "thing" (without committing myself to what the thing is) that "exists" in the space immediately surrounding the target person. This thing is not built of any known physical energies, yet it has a more "substantial" or "objective" kind of existence than simply a psychological construct that the person carries around. Another way of saying this might be to say that it exists on a different "level" or a different "plane." I am hesitant to use those words, since they tend to be popularly used in such ambiguous ways.

Again we have the same research questions as with respect to other kinds of aura. How is it detectable, what kind of conditions optimize detectability? Can you detect by any kind of instruments? What are the factors affecting the detectability of this sort of thing? Not only environmental factors, that will make it easier or harder to see, but psychological factors. Do some people have practically undetectable kinds of aura? Do other people have auras that are very easily detectable? What kind of people show this kind of variation? These are all questions that we eventually have to do research on.

Also, what are the characteristics of the observer that make possible the detection of this? How does the psychic detect it? This is one of the main things that I am going to come back to later because it's a very difficult problem. Again, the correlation of the psychic aura with the target person's characteristics is another large area that we are going to have to begin investigating.

We might ask questions also eventually about the *function* of the psychical aura. If it exists, what does it do for the person? What good is it? What disadvantages, if any, might we have? How do you train people to sense their own aura, possibly to enhance its functions? Or to eliminate undesirable functions, etc.?

In studying the psychical aura we come to a very difficult methodological problem. Since you must postulate some kind of extrasensory ability to detect it, how do you keep that extrasensory ability from picking up other, non-auric, characteristics of the observer which may be falsely attributed to the aura?

Going back to this doorway test, a way of starting to get at some of these problems, the *physical* aura would be instrumentally detectable in the doorway test, and the *psychical* aura should also be detectable by a talented psychic. The *psychological* aura would not: it is only a construct in the mind of a person, so it is not going physically to occupy the space around the edge of a doorway. The target person's position could be clairvoyantly detected, however, so it is conceivable that a psychic could reliably tell you when a person was and was not at the edge of that doorway, but falsely attribute it to seeing the psychical aura. As we do not know how to eliminate clairvoyance at any given time, we do not know how to deal with this possible confounding.

The Projected Aura

The fourth kind of aura I will call the *projected* aura. I use *projected* in the psychological and psychiatric sense of the term projection, meaning that you have an experience which exists only *within* your mind but you (falsely) classify it as a *perception* of the outside world. You project this thing into the outside world: nothing is out there, but you think it is there. This is quite distinct from the psychical aura: the psychical aura *is* there in some fashion.

We then can define the projected aura as something which is not out there at all: it exists only in the mind of the *observer*. The psychological aura, by contrast, existed only in the mind of the *target person*, although it could exist in other people's minds if he convinced them of it through persuasion.

The immediate reaction of many people to the concept of a projected aura is usually to think: "Oh, it's just an *error*. It's just a hallucination." But that is not the point I want to emphasize about it. The projected aura may or may not be a very *useful* source of information for the observer, even though it has no "objective" existence.

The way we might think of this process of experiencing the projected aura is this. The observer looks at the target person, and picks up various physical, and behavioural characteristics from seeing him. He may also receive an information input, to varying degrees, from his own *psychic* faculties, which may range from zero information to a great deal of information. Then, somewhere on an unconscious level, these inputs are transformed into a mental image and delivered to consciousness so that he "sees" an aura surrounding the target person. This projected aura may have "valid" characteristics. Depending on how good his observation of the target person's physical characteristics was, and/or the quality of the psychical information input, this projected aura may be a very *useful* and *valid* indication of the status of the target person.

We can thus treat the projected aura as an *information display system*. It may be a way in which certain kinds of information are presented to, "sensed" by an observer. It is an arbitrary way. Another person might never see auras: he might have an image, when he looks at a target person, of a scroll over their heads with things written on it. So one of the questions, in studying the projected aura, is, how *good* is the information coming through? At one extreme, if there is no psychical input, no clairvoyant input giving you extrasensory information about the person, and the only information the observer has is the physical and behavioural characteristics of the target person, then we are dealing with an interesting display but one that cannot really add any information over and above what you could get from simply carefully observing the actual target person. On the other hand, if there is psychical information input, there may be considerable information brought to the observer's consciousness in this fashion which might not be available otherwise. This is the observer's way of expressing himself.

The observer is, however, making an error in attributing his own information display process to something that exists in the outside world. A good example of this, for instance, with respect to "instruments," is the Kilner goggles. These are a pair of lenses coated with an organic dye which supposedly allows one to see auras. Ellison measured the optical transmission characteristics of the Kilner goggles. He found that the transmission was very good in the *far* red and the *far* violet. Since the human eye is not a perfect optical instrument, it will not focus the extreme ends of the visible spectrum perfectly, so there is an optical fringe created around anything viewed because these two extremes are being focused at slightly different places on the retina, and you don't have the information in the middle range of the visible spectrum to mask this lack of focus. So persons who put on Kilner goggles and see a fringe around people and say, "I see the aura," are seeing the *projected* aura. They are mistaking the malfunctioning of their visual system for something that exists in the environment.

Another instance of the projected aura, that is now occurring quite commonly in today's culture, occurs with people taking psychedelic drugs. I well remember the first time I took mescaline. I saw beautiful auras around people. And then I noticed that not only were they around people, but they were around objects, and then pretty soon they just came loose from everything and floated off through the air! It became rather clear to me that what I was seeing were changes in my optical system that were producing fringes of coloured lights everywhere, rather than something that could be attributed to the external visual objects.

Probably the drug effect is producing a projected aura by altering the nature of visual information processing. Possibly it is increasing the user's sensitivity to other types of aura. In any case, psychedelic drugs may provide an interesting avenue of research on the aura.

The Observer

Let us now consider the opposite end of the process, the observer himself. We tend naively to take our perception for granted. We all walk around thinking that we see what's out there. If there is one thing we have learned from modern research in this area, it is that perception is one of the most complicated processes imaginable. We take tremendous numbers of physical energies of various sorts, perform an immense number of mental operations on them, and end up with a mental construct that may be fairly far removed from the actual physical world.

This process provides a reasonable approximation of the real world for our ordinary life. We can see this blur of sensations coming down the street, we realize that it is a car, and we should not step out in front of that. Our mental construct is quite useful, it keeps us from getting run over.

Because of the complexity of perception, I suspect that in beginning to study the processes of the observer we may be reaching the most difficult area of study in this whole process of talking about seeing the aura. We know there are immense differences between people as observers in just the general sense of "observer." Some people are very poor observers in the sense that their observational processes are very much controlled by their needs, their past histories, etc. They pretty much see what they want to see. If they want to see the world as an unfriendly place, they see unfriendly actions all round them. If they are optimistic, they see people doing nice things all the time. Good observers tend to be people who have most of their needs satisfied so that these needs no longer interfere with their perception. They tend just to respond to what is there, they do not have to label it good or bad, pleasant or unpleasant. They can be more passive about it, simply reporting what they see.

Most of us, of course, are neither terribly bad observers with most of our perceptions determined by our needs, or good observers who can function without this. We are somewhere in-between. Still, to a large extent, especially in marginal areas of perception, where the stimulus is not obvious, it is very easy to see what you want to see. It is very easy to take the multitude of stimuli coming into yourself and all of us and to organize them into a pattern which fits your belief system, whatever your belief system may be.

Now when we deal with someone looking at the aura, this problem is very important: how do we know when we are getting a good report of what is "out there," and how do we know when we are primarily getting a report of the person's experience which reflects mainly his own belief system, his own special way of processing information which has only a tangential or zero relationship to whatever might or might not be "out there?" This is the problem of evaluating the usefulness of the aura reading. How valid is the information?

I think it would be very worthwhile at this time if I took a couple of minutes to describe a technique which has been developed in parapsychology, to give you an *objective* assessment of how much paranormal information you get from a psychometric reading, since it is directly applicable to evaluating the usefulness of aura readings. How do you objectively evaluate this?

The first thing that should be clear is that a single person cannot make an objective evaluation. His own belief system will alter what he wants to do. Some people, if they want to believe in a psychic, might hear the psychic say, "This man is a human being," and if the person wants to believe he'll say: "Yeah, right on, what fantastic psychic powers!" Another psychic might say, correctly: "You have a brother with two heads who lives in Hong Kong." And someone who doesn't want to believe may say: "Well, a lot of people have brothers with two heads who live in Hong Kong: it's probably coincidence." What is a reasonable assessment for one person is absolutely ridiculous to a second person. A given person's judgments on the accuracy of a psychic reading this way, the paranormality of the information, is usually going to be terribly subjective.

There was a technique, developed some years ago, but still not widely used, called the Pratt-Birge technique, which gets around the problem of subjectivity of evaluation entirely. To evaluate the paranormality of *any* kind of psychic reading, be it aura reading, psychometry reading, or the like, you start with a *sample* of persons who will each have a reading. To describe a typical experiment, you might start with locks of hair. Something like this eliminates one problem: there is no physical contact with the person, so you have eliminated the problem of valid information about the person arising from their physical characteristics alone. A lock of hair in an envelope presents very little useful *physical* information to a sensitive about what kind of person that human being is. So you start essentially with only some kind of token object, or just a name of a person, or an aura sticking around the doorway, or something like that, and you use, let's say, ten different persons, and your sensitive gives you a reading on each one of these. He says, "This is a man of such and such an age. He does such and such for a living." He gives various kinds of information. Some of it will be rather specific, and it might be right or it might be wrong.

Now if you simply gave those readings to each of the ten people and say: "This is what was said about you. How accurate is it?" you would still be dealing with a purely subjective evaluation. Instead, what you do is to take *all* the information from all ten readings, and put it together in one big heap. You just type it all out into single statements of information, with no indication that this was intended for this person and this was intended for that person. You take the whole battery of information, you give this to all the people, and you say, "Some of these statements were intended to be about you. Some of them were intended to be about others. I'm not telling you which. But you should treat every statement *as if* it were intended to be a description of you, and rate it as true or false." You can use a more elaborate rating system if you want to, to allow for the improbability of various kinds of thing.

You then get all this information back, and you break the code showing which statements were intended for which people and which were not and you can then statistically assess whether, at one extreme, the readings are equally right for everybody. Such a result is most simply interpreted on a null hypothesis of chance, that you are dealing essentially with generalities, there is really no specific information. Or, you can assess at the other extreme, whether statements specifically intended for a given person were right more frequently for that person than they were for other people. And you end up with a statistical figure on this that tells you whether you are dealing with paranormal information.

The beauty of this technique, and the refinements that could be done on it, is that you can find out when you have a "good" sensitive, in the sense of someone who is really giving you information about what is out there, and when you have a poor sensitive who is primarily telling you about his own belief system. Again, this assumes you can filter out the information from the physical characteristics of the person. If you're doing an aura reading and the sensitive is looking at the target person, you're clearly going to get very significant scores with a Pratt-Birge analysis, but these are going to be a matter of what you can tell about a person simply from looking at his physical characteristics. But this sort of technique can begin to tell us how much paranormal information there is in the phenomena we study. Then, once you can develop a number of good sensitives who are giving you primarily paranormal information, then you can begin to use them in a calibrated way, or as a known good observer, and begin to study other kinds of auric properties.

Summary

Let me just summarize by saying that if you ask a question, "Is the aura real?" you are asking much too simple a question. Which aura? The physical one? The psychical one? The psychological one? The projected aura? Under what kinds of condition, with what kinds of observers? Real to *whom*? To an instrument, to a human being, to an animal which you might train as an observer?

So, you cannot just ask whether an aura is "real." You have got to specify what kind of aura you are talking about, under what kinds of condition, etc. What I have tried to do here is to indicate some of the methodological and logical complexities in the field we have been discussing and to point out the need for distinguishing these things, as well as to suggest some methods we can begin to use to get at these phenomena.

18

ENERGY FIELDS AND MEDICAL DIAGNOSIS

Shafica Karagulla

Dr. Shafica Karagulla, a neuropsychiatrist, has extensively studied "sensitives" who claim to see swirls of energy around people. One of these sensitives, Diane, as Karagulla describes, has an astounding diagnostic ability. The following is an account of a continuing research effort.

* * *

The fellowship from the Pratt Foundation made it possible for me to plan a long-range program of research. I had to choose projects that could be done with a minimum of cost, but I was determined not to let this hinder me. There were a few problems. Most of the people I considered good HSP [Higher Sense Perception] subjects were leading a full and busy life in their own businesses or professions. They would have little time to give to an experimental program. There were no funds available to recompense people for their time.

Eventually I arranged a program of research with a few of the most outstandingly gifted individuals. Three of them gave considerable time without charge and planned their own schedules as far as possible to fit in with my experiments. Two of these were presidents of corporations and the third held a professional job which made heavy demands on her time and energy.

Diane, president of a corporation and with a family to care for, arranged to give me twelve hours a week. She is one of the most gifted individuals I have ever encountered. She has control of her gifts and can use them efficiently at any time. Her clairvoyant observations are reliable and consistent.

In order to make clear the experiments in medical diagnosis which follow, I must explain in general what Diane "sees." She can see the physical organs of the body and any pathology or disturbance in function. She has not studied medicine or physiology and often her descriptions are those one would expect of a layman. These descriptions are accurate and clear and easily translate into medical terms. Medical diagnosis has proved that Diane is correct and accurate in what she sees.

It is the other things that Diane "sees" which continue to fascinate me. She observes a "vital or energy body or field" which sub-stands the dense physical body, interpenetrating it like a sparkling web of light beams. This web of light frequencies is in constant movement and apparently looks somewhat like the lines of light on a television screen when a picture is not in focus. This energy body extends in and through the dense physical body and for an inch or two beyond the body and is a replica of the physical body. She insists that any disturbance in the physical structure itself is preceded and later accompanied by disturbances in this energy body or field. Within this energy body or pattern of frequencies she observes eight major vortices of force and many smaller vortices. As she describes it, energy moves in and out of these vortices, which look like spiral cones. Seven of these major vortices are directly related to the different glands of the body. She describes them as also being related to any pathology in the physical body in their general area. The spiral cones of energy that make up these vortices may be fast or slow, rhythmical or jerky. She sometimes see breaks in the energy pattern. Each major vortex, as she describes it more minutely, is made up of a number of lesser spiral cones of energy and each major vortex differs in the number of these spiral cones.

Five of these macro-vortices are located in a line along the spine. There is one at the base of the spine, one approximately midway between the pubic bone and the

navel, one at the navel, one at the level of the mid-
sternum near the heart area and one near the larynx or
Adam's apple. There is another macro-vortex on the left
side of the body in the area of the spleen and pancreas.
This one does not seem to be connected with the spinal
pattern of vortices. There are two other macro-vortices,
one approximately where the eyebrows meet and one at
the top of the head. There is a ninth smaller vortex at
the back of the head in the vicinity of the medulla ob-
longata.

Diane describes the energy vortex at the base of the
spine as having a direct connection with the adrenal
glands. According to her description it is made up of four
smaller spiral cones of whirling energy with the sharp
points of the cones fitting into a center point. If there is
any disturbance in this central point or core, then she
looks for some pathology in the area. Breaks or disturbances in the spiral cone have to do with some function of
the physical body in that area. If any of these major
vortices show a dullness or irregularity or "leak" in this
central point or core, she looks for some serious pathology in the physical body in the area. If the pattern of the
cone of energy is out of rhythm or shows a "break or
crack" she finds that it is related to a problem of function
in the area. Each of the major vortices which Diane observes has its own characteristic number of spiral cones of
energy which form the total macro-vortex. In each case
the major vortex, as she observes it, presents a mandal-
la pattern. In the early experiments with Diane I chose
patients of my own with clearly confirmed medical diag-
noses. Then I asked Diane to observe the patient and
describe in as complete detail as possible the total physical
condition. Not even the name of the patient was given to
her. She described the actual physical condition which
turned out to be entirely accurate in all the cases. In
addition, she described the appearance of the energy
body or field and the vortices of force.

I began to realize that I must first have reports on the
appearance of this energy body in healthy people in
order to have a basis for comparison in the case of dis-

ease. Day after day Diane gave her report on one healthy individual after another, describing the energy body, the vortices of force and the condition of physical organs, glands, nerves and tissues. Eventually I began to have a fairly clear picture of what Diane saw in states of health.

A friend of mine and her husband agreed to be guinea pigs on my program for evaluating healthy people. On the first evaluation Diane described them both as being very healthy specimens. A year later the husband stopped by one day, and I suggested that Diane do a second examination. I had done this on a number of occasions so that I could compare evaluations of the same individual. Diane was somewhat hesitant about discussing the total picture while my friend was still present. She made notes and gave me the rest of the evaluation after he had left. She explained to me that there were certain disruptions and disturbances in the energy body which had not been present a year previous. She described this condition and said to her this meant that within a year to eighteen months my friend would have a very serious physical disorder and a serious hip condition.

I had begun to realize that Diane's observations even in predicting the onset of a disease were pretty accurate. I discussed this with the wife. Since there was nothing we could tell him from a medical point of view, we decided not to discuss it with him. I did make a point of encouraging them both to take a trip around the world which they had been planning for many years. Personally, I felt that in case Diane should be right, they should enjoy life while he was in good health. Within eighteen months he had developed Parkinson's disease which has become progressively worse and he was hospitalized for an operation due to a serious hip condition.

Diane insisted that this was not precognition. The energy web or body showed the condition clearly many months before it became apparent in the physical body. As I continued to work with Diane she was able to repeatedly predict the onset of a disease or to indicate the progress of a disease by what she saw in the energy body or web. She always described this energy pattern as intimately related to the physical body at every point.

The total structure of this energy body which Diane and other individuals see shows the same kind of variation as different types of physical bodies in different individuals. For example, the whole web of energy may appear to her as tightly woven or loosely woven, as coarse or fine, as dull or bright. It may extend as much as two inches beyond the physical body or less than an inch. In conditions of disease, it may show a wide range of disturbances. There may be loss in the energy field, breaks in the pattern, tiny whirlpools of energy that have broken off from the normal stream, gaps in the web, or a jumble of lines of force like scar tissue. All of these things Diane relates to conditions in the physical body in consistent and accurate observation.

When we had a large number of case studies on normal individuals I was ready to return to observations on people who were ill. I decided to handle two groups of patients, those whose medical history was well known to me and patients about whose medical record I knew nothing. In the case of the latter group, I arranged to have access to the medical record after I had Diane's evaluations. This would exclude the possibility that Diane was in any way reading my mind.

I am always amused when, after some very convincing experiment, the doubter says, "Oh, but the person was just reading your mind." After all, reading someone else's mind is an HSP ability of a high order. Nevertheless, in these experiments I wanted to rule out any possibility that Diane could be reading my mind. If I did not know anything about the diagnosis of some of the patients there would be no way for Diane to tune in on what I knew. Certainly Diane's description of an energy body with an orderly relatedness to the physical body was an idea totally alien to my own thinking and my medical training.

It seemed important to begin with patients whose medical record was well-known to me so that I could establish some kind of a norm for equating what Diane saw with my own medical observations and terminology. The first group I selected were patients whom I had studied or treated while working as an associate of Dr. Penfield at the Montreal Neurological Institute in Canada. I had a complete medical history on these patients with full documentation on their physical, neurological and psychiatric condition. Some of these patients had had brain tumors, others had had parts of the brain removed by Dr. Penfield for the relief of epilepsy.

My method with Diane was to have her sit facing the patient, who was fully clothed, with about twelve feet between them. I sat beside Diane, also facing the patient. I took notes and asked questions, going through an established routine upon which we had decided. We started at the top of the head with Diane observing and describing both the condition of the energy body and the condition of the physical body. We moved down through the torso to the feet. We recorded any malfunction or pathology which she saw in the physical body. I also took a minute description of what she saw in the energy body and how she related it to the physical.

Early in the experimental work with Diane I endeavored to record all the variations that Diane could observe in the energy body. This made it possible to make up a systematic form to guide us in the observation. In addition to my notes I took a tape recording of each evaluation. The observation of each patient took from three to four hours. I went over each point in her observations minutely for further clarification.

Diane seemed a little hesitant about telling me what she saw with some of the first patients, especially when parts of the brain were missing, because she thought this was impossible. On the first case she thought there must be something wrong with her own usually reliable observation. As we established good working methods and an easy rapport, Diane felt at ease and the work went very well. I assured her that any mistakes would be just as valuable as the things that were entirely accurate. As time went on I was amazed at the accuracy of her diagnosis where actual physical conditions were concerned.

One of my patients, Miss Jay, had just arrived in New York on a visit from Montreal, and I immediately seized upon the opportunity to have Diane observe her. Miss Jay had suffered from temporal lobe epilepsy. She had also exhibited periodic moods of violence and aggression between her seizures which had made her a dangerous person. I had been present when Dr. Wilder Penfield had performed two operations on her brain for the relief of temporal lobe epilepsy. The right temporal lobe of the brain had been removed. Full documentation on this case was in my file. The patient had improved considerably following the operation and was able to live a more nearly normal life.

I placed Miss Jay in a comfortable chair in my office, and when Diane came in for the afternoon's work we proceeded with our observations. Diane did not know the patient's name nor did she know anything about her medical history. When Diane observed the energy field around the head she said that it seemed to be out too far on the right side. The energy field around the head area seemed to her to be "thicker" in texture on the right as compared to the left side. This thickness or opacity she described as penetrating into the brain itself in the prefrontal region. The energy pattern was jerky and irregular.

When I asked Diane to describe the physical brain she seemed puzzled by what she saw and rather hesitantly said, "On the right side there is a bare patch with nothing in between. The energy has to jump across." I asked her to indicate the general area by pointing it out on the patient's head. She pointed out the correct area.

I asked Diane to look at the energy vortex at the top of the head. She described one of the tiny spirals of energy as drooping downward like the drooping petal of a flower instead of standing upward in what we had come to designate as the normal pattern. This indicated to

Diane that the brain energy pattern showed a long-standing disturbance. As she put it, "The energy pattern in this person's brain wasn't quite right from the beginning." Diane went on to say, "The energy pattern in the brain is erratic. Instead of an orderly pattern the lines of energy crisscross in a confused jumble." She thought that the person must have "disturbances in her consciousness," and that she could become confused or unconscious.

As we continued to observe the brain of the patient and its energy pattern, Diane remarked that the left side of the brain had to work faster to compensate for the lack on the right side. As she looked at the energy field she described the right side of the brain as showing short, jerky wave patterns and the left side as showing longer wave patterns. Diane was puzzled by the bare patch in the physical brain and I did not explain to her until we had completed our observations that part of the brain had been removed.

We moved to the throat area and I encouraged Diane to feel free to express any opinions of her own concerning what she saw. When she looked at the thyroid area she described an irregular energy pattern which was sometimes tight and constricting and rapid in movement and at other times very slow. She said, "There are times when this person tends to scream with wild and uncontrollable force." With encouragement Diane volunteered some further information. She said that the patient was very strong willed and wished to dominate people. She felt shut-in and restricted and there was a lot of emotional disturbance.

I have given only the highlights of the afternoon's observations. Diane was correct in her findings regarding the patient's actual physical condition. My psychiatric findings on the patient two years previous confirmed Diane's opinion on her emotional behavior. Miss Jay still showed the desire to dominate and she still showed considerable emotional disturbance though not to the extent of being a danger to society. As she sat in the easy chair in my office she was quiet and controlled and to all outward appearances she looked healthy.

For many weeks Diane continued to observe patients whose physical conditions and medical histories were well known to me. I began to get a clearer understanding of how Diane saw the physical body and the energy body in states of disease or malfunction. Her observations of physical conditions correlated with amazing accuracy with the medical diagnosis. Although I could not evaluate her findings regarding the energy body, at least I began to find a consistent correlation of these findings with the observations of the physical body. The fact that there was a consistent and logical pattern certainly gave credence to what Diane said.

About this time a friend of mine asked if she could bring Dorothy Thompson, the well-known columnist, for dinner and to discuss Higher Sense Perception. During the course of the evening Dorothy Thompson told me that her father had had very marked healing ability. This ability seemed to be concentrated in his hands. She told me that for some time she had felt an urge to write his life story. My studies in Higher Sense Perception had intrigued her and she was interested to know whether I had tested people with healing gifts. She was also interested to know whether I had any explanation of such ability. We talked about Diane's observations of people with healing ability. I explained to her that Diane saw certain patterns in the energy field of individuals with healing gifts. She was eager to meet Diane and volunteered to be a guinea pig herself for one of my evaluating sessions with Diane.

A few days later Dorothy Thompson arrived for one of our regular sessions. In this case she was receiving a medical evaluation. As it turned out, Diane also gave a good deal of information about Dorothy Thompson's gifts and abilities. Diane did not know who the subject was and had no information about her. In fact, I had no information about her medical history.

Since we had a limited amount of time, I asked Diane to

take a look at the total energy field. If there was anything that did not appear to be normal, we would confine our observation to that area.

The one area that did not appear to be normal was in the abdominal region. Diane observed local changes in this area that did not appear in a healthy condition. She described the energy field in this area as appearing to be "wilted" and "broken into fragments." This was more marked around the umbilical region. To Diane this indicated a serious problem in the physical body already in evidence. The remaining overall field was wider than that of most people. The energy moved at a faster rate and was brighter than it appeared in the average person. Diane remarked that the subject had always been a person with a great deal of energy and vitality.

I asked Diane to describe what she saw in the physical body in the abdominal area. She said, "The colon is blocked. The blockage is in the left upper area of the abdomen near the spleen area." I was somewhat taken aback by this. The subject had been at my home a few days before and had eaten normally. Medically, I knew that an intestinal obstruction resulted in symptoms of vomiting, pain and discomfort. Dorothy Thompson had made no mention of any health problem. I asked Diane to point out the exact spot in the patient's abdomen where she saw the block. She pointed out the spot which she had already described.

We moved on to some further observations. Diane remarked that although the subject had always had great vitality, she constantly pushed herself beyond her physical capacity, and her adrenals were under a constant state of stress. She added that the subject had recently had a great emotional shock which had also affected her physically. The subject's husband had died a few months previously, but this Diane did not know.

When we had completed the session and Diane had left, Dorothy Thompson turned to me and said, "May I use the telephone? I have to call my doctor." She went on to explain that she had been a little late in arriving because she had been delayed in the X-ray Department at the hospital that morning. Her doctor thought there might be an obstruction somewhere in her intestinal tract. She wanted to find out whether there was any report on the X-rays.

Three days later Dorothy Thompson underwent a surgical operation for an obstruction in the colon in the exact area indicated by Diane. In this case, Diane gave a diagnosis as accurate as that of an X-ray machine, and it was almost immediately confirmed by surgery.

After Dorothy Thompson was out of the hospital we had another session with Diane and recorded her observations. Diane said that the blockage which she had previously seen in the colon was absent. There was some improvement locally. She felt that the subject had had a shock to the nervous system and the total energy field did not look as vital.

In research of any kind, single cases are very interesting and certainly indicate direction for further study, but they are not conclusive. In the next two years we made scores of case history studies which I have in my medical files. Since Diane seemed to be especially expert in observing changes in the macro-vortices of energy related to the endocrine glands, I arranged for us to continue our research in the outpatients' department of the Endocrine Clinic of a large New York hospital. I selected patients at random and later abstracted the medical data from the case records of the hospital. Our routine procedure was to sit quietly and as unobtrusively as possible in a corner of the waiting room of the outpatients' clinic. I pointed out a patient and Diane proceeded to make her observation while I took notes. When the observations were completed I took the patient's name and later went over his or her case record.

One of the early cases was a patient with Paget's disease. Neither Diane nor myself knew anything about the patient's condition at the time we made the observations. I simply selected one of the patients sitting in the waiting room a little over twelve feet away from us. Diane's report on the patient, as was customary, included a description of the general energy body, the vortices of force and then the actual physical condition. Diane often gives her descriptions in terms of color along with the other descriptions I have mentioned. As she looked at the energy body of the patient, she noted that the vortex of energy located at the throat showed a gray color with red specks. She described these cones of energy as moving at different rhythms with an irregular slowing down and speeding up. In the normal person, Diane sees these spiral cones of energy at the throat vortex as blue-grey in color and all moving at the same steady rhythm. In the patient under observation, Diane described the center of this vortex of energy as being a dull gray and showing an irregular slow and fast beat.

When she observed the physical body of the patient she said that the thyroid appeared "dead looking." Quite a bit of it was not there. The energy of the parathyroids was "flickering," and she was sure the person had a disease of the parathyroids. The trouble was more on the right side than on the left. When she looked at the patient's head, the skull on the right side, which I identified as the parietal region, appeared thinned out. The same characteristic showed to a less extent at the back of the head. As she looked at the rest of the body, the bones of the legs and spine looked "crummy" to her. She explained that normal bones look harder and thicker. She came back to the right side of the head, somewhat puzzled to explain what she saw. She said, "Not enough bone is present. It does not seem to be complete. It is thinner and granular."

She found the liver slow in function and the adrenals were working too fast. The right kidney was hardly functioning at all and had the same "crummy stuff" in it. She described the left kidney as functioning only fairly well, and it seemed to have some kind of "soft stones" in it. She saw the same "crummy stuff" in the wall of the gut, and she said that the intestines were slow in their function.

The medical report on this patient gave Paget's disease as the clinical diagnosis. X-rays showed thinness of the skull on the right side in the parietal region and at the back of the head. Part of the thyroid had been removed and the right parathyroid. The left parathyroid was still present. The right kidney was hardly functioning at all, the X-rays indicated what appeared to be stones in the left kidney. There was a mass the size of a fist in the colon. The patient complained of general weakness and pain in the bones of the spine and legs. Diane's observations, although they were in a layman's language, correlated very accurately with the medical diagnosis.

A few days later we selected another patient at random in the waiting room at the Endocrine Clinic. This patient I discovered later had Graves' disease. Diane described the energy vortex at the throat as being too active. She saw red color in this vortex along with a dull gray color. All this meant poor and erratic function of the thyroid as far as Diane was concerned. She also described an erratic rhythm in the energy flow.

When she looked at the thyroid itself she saw it as spongy and soft in texture. It did not look normal or healthy and was larger than it should be. The right side of the thyroid was not functioning as well as the left. The parathyroids appeared normal. Diane said that the patient had a tendency to become dizzy and had periods of great exhaustion.

The medical diagnosis showed Graves' disease with an enlarged thyroid, the right lobe being larger. The patient suffered from rapid pulse, weakness, exhaustion and nervous tremors. The complete medical diagnosis and treatment included a more detailed medical discussion, but this summed up the medical findings. Diane's observations followed very accurately what many weeks of observation and testing had revealed.

Day after day Diane and I followed our routine of selecting a patient at random with no knowledge of his medical background. We sat quietly in the waiting room of the Endocrine Clinic while she made the observations and I wrote down the notes. From time to time I asked questions to clarify some point or to get a more complete description. The case histories in my files grew in volume and I continued to be amazed at the acuracy of Diane's findings.

One afternoon I pointed out a patient in chair number five and Diane began to describe an abnormal condition of the pituitary gland. She found the vortex of energy in the immediate vicinity as slow in movement followed by bursts of hyper-activity of short duration. The vortex of energy showed a gray color with specks and flashes of orange which she declared as most abnormal.

When she looked at the pituitary gland itself, her description was fairly detailed. "Half of it looks bright and half of it looks dull. Part of it seems dead and hardly functioning at all. Part of it is functioning too fast. There seems to be spasmodic over-stimulation. The gland may have a growth, but the energy pattern I see at the vortex tells me it is not cancer. There is a spasmodic over-stimulation which seems to cause too much growth. The adrenal glands are affected by the pituitary."

Looking further at the patient's physical condition, she said that the patient had diabetes. She was puzzled by this because she insisted that there was nothing wrong with the pancreas in this patient. She had observed a number of diabetic cases with me and had always noted that the pancreas was involved.

The medical diagnosis showed acromegaly, a disease of the pituitary which causes increased size in the hands and feet. The patient had had thirty X-ray treatments of the pituitary region. He had diabetes mellitus which is associated with a disturbance of the pituitary rather than the pancreas.

The following day we decided, before we entered the waiting room of the clinic, we would take the patient in the third chair down from the door. It turned out that this patient also had acromegaly. Diane described the energy vortex in the pituitary as gray in color with flecks of red and orange. The rhythm was slow and fast in irregular spurts.

The pituitary itself showed a condition similar to the

patient of the previous day. The thyroid function Diane described as normal and the parathyroids low in function. The ovaries and the uterus were absent and she said the patient had diabetes.

The medical diagnosis showed that the patient suffered from acromegaly with the accompanying symptoms. She had had a hysterectomy with the uterus and ovaries removed. She also had diabetes mellitus. She had had thirty X-ray treatments for the pituitary condition.

The next day we selected chair number seven before we entered the clinic. We sat down quietly and began our observations on the patient immediately. Diane saw a disturbed pattern of energy in the vortex at the throat with an irregular rhythm and gray color. The vortex at the pituitary was also disturbed and the energy vortex at the solar plexus.

When Diane looked at the physical body itself she described low function of the thyroid. She went on to say, "The pituitary gland is not there. It is out. The pancreas is not functioning and the adrenals are functioning very poorly. It seems that the periphery of the adrenals is not functioning. The breasts have been affected but they are not there now. There is not enough energy going through the spine from the waist down. She has trouble with her legs."

The medical report on the patient said that the pituitary glands had been removed and the patient was being given pituitrin and cortisone. The breasts had been removed because of cancer. She had had an operation on her back and decompression of the cord to relieve pains in her legs, numbness and difficulty in emptying the bladder. The patient was still taking cortisone, pituitrin and thyroid.

On our next visit to the clinic we decided to choose the ninth patient from the door for observation. As was our usual procedure, Diane first observed the energy field and the vortices of force. She found the greatest disturbance in the energy vortex over the solar plexus area. The movement of energy was irregular and jerky and it appeared to her that there was a leakage of energy from the center of the vortex. The vortex itself was gray in color, varying from dark gray to light gray with a little green and orange. This gray color in the energy vortex always indicates trouble in that area.

As Diane looked at the physical level, she remarked that the left adrenal had been removed and that the right adrenal was not normal and seemed to be lopsided. The outer part appeared to her to be overactive and the inner part underactive. The left ovary was not functioning. The kidneys were slowed down. The pituitary seemed dark and she thought that perhaps it had been removed. There seemed to be no function.

The medical findings showed a diagnosis of Cushing's Syndrome, a disturbance in the adrenals relating to the pituitary. The left adrenal had been removed and part of the right adrenal. The pituitary had not been removed but was seriously involved. The exact degree of function was not determined.

I had been eager to have Kay and Diane work together on some of these cases, each making an independent observation which we could afterwards compare. Since Kay senses or feels in her own body whatever conditions exist in the patient, I felt that this would be an interesting project. Kay arranged to be in New York for several months and to work with Diane and me.

The first morning Kay and Diane arrived with me at the outpatients' department of the Endocrine Clinic. Kay knew, as Diane did, that they were to make observations on patients with endocrine disturbances. While I went to talk to one of the internes, they sat on the bench in the outpatients' department. Kay, who is always an eager beaver, decided to make a few trial runs on patients who were sitting in a large room facing her. Finally she turned to Diane and said, "I thought we were seeing patients with glandular disturbances. Every time I tune in to feel the condition of one of these patients facing us, I get a terrible pain in the rectum. I don't know what is wrong."

Diane, who had been to the clinic before, laughed and

said, "Look at the sign above the door. We're facing the rectal clinic. The endocrine clinic is behind us."

Kay's mistake was just as valuable as any of her other observations. She was fully expecting to feel discomfort or pain in the pituitary area or the throat area or areas associated with the adrenals and in spite of herself she kept getting a pain in the rectum. We had a good laugh when Diane told me the story.

I had selected a number of thyroid cases for observation. Some of these were hyper-functioning, some were hypo-functioning, some were cancerous and others full of small nodules. Other patients had the thyroid removed and were receiving replacement therapy. I had also selected patients with pituitary disturbances, disturbances of the pancreas and some with adrenal disturbances. Kay was to write down her impressions without consulting Diane.

Kay was invariably correct with regard to which endocrine gland was involved. She tuned in to the patient and felt whatever discomfort the patient was feeling at that time. She could tell me whether the basic problem was the thyroid, the pituitary, the pancreas or the adrenals. She also sensed accompanying disturbances but was unable to describe the exact condition of a gland or organ.

Diane always saw the physical condition exactly as it was and described the energy pattern accompanying it. She knew whether there was a cancerous condition or a non-malignant growth. She could tell whether there was a disturbance in function or a pathological condition and her observations correlated very accurately with the medical findings when I compared them. She was also very clear about the removal of a gland or a part of a gland. In all these studies in the endocrine clinic I had no knowledge of the medical record of the patients until after the sensitives had made their observations.

Diane proved to be a constant source of amazement to me. I discovered that not only was she aware of the condition of the physical body and its energy field but she also saw an emotional or sentient field. According to her description this field extends from a foot to eighteen inches from the periphery of the body and is ovoid in form. In this field she sees colors and energy patterns which indicate emotional states and conditions.

One afternoon Diane arrived for some of our experimental work and I was late finishing an interview with a former patient who had insisted on seeing me. The particular patient was an extremely self-centered individual who actually had very little wrong with her. She always insisted upon getting as much attention as possible from everybody in her vicinity. I am inclined to be rather impatient with people who seem to want attention and who are not truly ill. I finally ushered the patient in question to the door, pleasantly and in my best professional manner. I was giving every appearance of being unruffled and in the best of moods. Knowing that Diane could see the emotional field, I turned to her and asked her what she thought of my present emotional state. She replied with her characteristic straightforwardness, "You are very exasperated and irritated. The patient annoyed you very much."

"How do you know?" I asked, somewhat taken aback that she had read me so clearly.

Diane laughed. "I see little red spots all over your emotional field, like measles."

I had to admit that she was correct. I concluded that it was difficult to hide anything from Diane, and that it was fortunate that her friends were not aware of this particular aspect of her HSP ability.

Another afternoon session turned out to be very interesting. The patient whom I had scheduled for Diane's evaluation was not able to come. Vicky had arrived from the West Coast shortly before Diane was due. She was very tired from a heavy schedule and had a bad case of laryngitis by the time she reached New York. I knew Vicky's medical history, so here was a guinea pig made to order in place of the patient who could not come. I asked Vicky to sit down in an easy chair, relax and say nothing while Diane made her observations. Diane arrived and we proceeded with our usual schedule. Vicky did not look ill to a casual observer. Diane immediately saw inflammation in the throat and larynx and was of the opinion that the subject had lost her voice. She remarked that the energy body was "droopy" and looked wilted. This indicated to Diane that the subject was suffering from temporary low vitality and extreme fatigue. There was a slight disturbance of function in the thyroid which showed as a fluctuation of its activity. It had probably been a lifelong condition. It was not really serious but the subject was probably aware of it.

When Diane observed the energy body she described the macro-vortex at the throat as having a slight leakage of energy at its center. This indicated that the throat area was a point of weakness and that the subject was liable to frequent throat infections. She probably had a chronic tendency to clear her throat.

When Diane looked at the heart area, the macro-vortex showed a slight variation in the rate of movement, indicating to Diane a tendency for the slowing down and speeding up of the circulation of the heart. I knew that Vicky had been subject to tachycardia from time to time. Looking at the physical heart itself, she said there was evidence of trouble with function several years previously; but this had been corrected and was no longer a problem. I was surprised that Diane observed this. I knew that Vicky had had mild attacks of angina several years previously at the time of her husband's death. She had apparently made a complete recovery. I had forgotten about the condition and so had Vicky. Diane was correct about the thyroid function and the tendency to throat infection and to clear the throat.

When we stopped for tea and a purely social discussion, she turned to my friend Vicky and remarked, "You have certain types of Higher Sense Perception." Since Vicky had some difficulty speaking and I was intrigued to know why Diane had said this, I pursued the inquiry. I asked Diane what kind of Higher Sense Perception Vicky had and how she knew.

"For one thing," said Diane, "she can see past events in history when she tries. She can also pick up pictures that other people have in their minds when they are describing a place or an event to her. If the individual's ability to picture things to himself is fuzzy or inadequate, she picks up a fuzzy or vague picture."

Then Diane turned to Vicky and said, "When you have visited historical sites in Europe and the Orient haven't they looked exactly as you expected?"

Vicky looked surprised. "Yes, when I come to think of it, they always have looked just as I imagined they would. Of course I must have seen photographs or read descriptions."

Diane persisted, "But there must have been places where you couldn't have seen a photograph beforehand." Vicky could recall a few. "Did they look exactly as you expected?" asked Diane. Vicky was sure they did.

"I must have read descriptions of them," she said, rather puzzled. Diane pointed out that if twenty different people read the same description they would have twenty different pictures in their minds, but Vicky always had the correct picture. As Vicky thought it over she came to the conclusion that probably Diane was right. In the normal process of living it had never occurred to her that other people did not get the correct and right image of a place or a historical site when they read about it. There had never been an occasion to discover that this was not the case.

Diane remarked that Vicky had two ways of thinking or two types of mental processes. One of these moved along with vivid mental pictures of what she read or heard. The other was an abstract line of thought that had no pictorial accompaniment. These two mental processes usually moved along simultaneously on two levels. Vicky was aware of this but considered it a usual and normal procedure and was astonished that Diane should consider it otherwise.

At this point I interrupted to ask Diane how she was

able to point out abilities of this type. Another of Diane's amazing talents came to light. When she saw certain connections between or among two or more of the macro-vortices of energy in the energy body, she knew that the individual had certain types of Higher Sense Perception. The particular type of HSP depended on the connections and the maro-vortices involved. Through years of observation she had come to correlate these patterns with the particular types of abilities. She explained that it was very much like circuitry in electricity. Different types of connections indicated the type of ability or HSP to look for or expect. She went on to say that Vicky had several other types of HSP, but we did not have time to go into further discussion and observations.

19

ARE PSYCHOENERGETIC PICTURES POSSIBLE?

William A. Tiller

William A. Tiller, professor of materials science at Stanford University, offers a critical appraisal of the Kirlian process. In the growing atmosphere of reflection now that Kirlian-mania seems to have peaked, Tiller's comments usher in a more critical and cautious phase of energy field research.

* * *

A form of high-voltage photography called Kirlian photography has recently triggered considerable interest. First developed by the Soviet scientist Semyon Kirlian, who studied the technique for more than 30 years, psychologists, psychiatrists, biologists and physicists now look on the technique as a unique way of observing energy states associated with living things. Some investigators in the U.S. are already trying to use it as a diagnostic tool to monitor the psychological and physiological conditions of their patients.

Early statements pointing to this technique as being able to photograph the "aura," seen heretofore only by clairvoyants, created a flurry of excitement in parapsychology. Even more extravagant claims have been made about the process based upon very little firsthand information and some wishful thinking by a few not-so-careful experimenters.

The photographs are taken without any light source and result from electric discharges between an object and an electrode. The simplest form is shown in Figure 1. An object to be photographed, such as a leaf or a coin, is placed between parallel metal plates of a capacitorlike electrode arrangement and separated by a small distance from a piece of photographic film (emulsion side towards the object). This is generally carried out at normal atmospheric and temperature conditions. Soviet studies have indicated that for a good picture a spacing of 0.01 nm to 1 mm should be maintained between the object and the film. To photograph a person's finger pad, the arrangement illustrated in Figure 2 is used. A third arrangement uses a transparent electrode upon which the finger pad is placed; the light generated in the discharge process is photographed from a remote position.

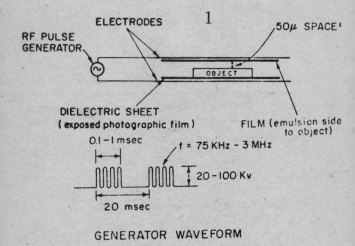

GENERATOR WAVEFORM

Figure 1   Simple Kirlian photographic equipment and waveform using capacitor plate configuration

The Soviets found that it was possible to detect and monitor electronically generated flares and bursts of light emitted from points on the living system or object. From the colour and intensity of the flares, the Soviet researchers said they could deduce relevant information concerning the physical, emotional and mental condition of a human subject. They reported that the technique has found meaningful use in agriculture, medicine, psychology and engineering.

Thelma Moss, at the University of California at Los Angeles, utilised the single electrode technique and 1-10 kHz pulses to study the effects of drugs and alcohol on the energy emission from finger pads. She has found some remarkable colour (white, blue, red, orange, yellow) and energy intensity effects. The red and blue photo on the cover is of a finger pad. She has also reported effects associated with damaging leaves of plants and the changes associated with their treatment by a healer (laying on of hands). Unfortunately, in these studies no precautions were taken to control either finger cleanliness or finger pressure on the film.

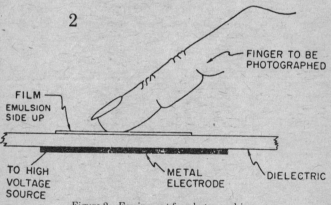

Figure 2   Equipment for photographing discharge from finger pad

Most other U.S. investigators have been using a similar technique and one pair have been studying energy changes on Kirlian photographs both before and after treatment of schizophrenics and alcoholics. Before treatment, both groups show a marked spatial fragmentation or annihilation of large portions of the normal emissions from the finger pad. In addition, the pattern of emission from the contact portion of the finger pad appears quite chaotic. After successful treatment, as indicated by conventional psychiatric criteria, one observes (a) the filling in of the emission pattern around the finger pad, (b) an enhancement of manifested energy intensity and (c) a more orderly and coherent fingerprint pattern on the contact portion of the photographs. Once again, no finger pad cleaning or pressure control procedures were instituted. The pulse length used in this study was 4 to 8 seconds.

Light generation mechanism

At Stanford, we conducted a number of experiments using a similar electrode configuration to Figure 2 and a high frequency power supply operating at 1 MHz. Single pulse discharges from both biological and metallic electrodes were found to occur from a network of points on the electrode surface. Multiple pulses were found to produce a superposition effect such that a uniform "aura" exposure appeared on the film.

During the fingertip studies, it was found that the photograph depended significantly on the electrode-film combination. Considerable variability occurred in these results as a consequence of the inability to repeatedly establish a well-defined and controlled discharge spacing and finger orientation.

Thus, we decided to restrict our initial studies to those where reliable information could be gained, and started by studying discharges between flat, polished metal electrodes.

All the photographs were found to reveal the same characteristic dot discharge pattern with relatively uniform dot spacing. However, in a number of photographs, large clear patches containing no dots were found. These patches disappeared when glass photographic plates instead of film were used.

Looking at Streamers

One has only to casually read L. B. Loeb's book *Electrical Coronas* (U. Calif. Press, 1965) to realise that we are dealing here with the corona discharge phenomenon called "streamers." In this process, a few electrons are first produced in the interelectrode space, are accelerated by the field and ionize the air molecules, yielding an exponential growth in the number of electrons and positive ions. The electrons sweep quickly toward the anode (positive) and the cluster of positive ions moves somewhat more slowly towards the cathode (negative). When the positive ion cluster in the air gap reaches a critical density, it strongly attracts the electrons so that a large number of recombination events occur and photons of light are generated to such a degree that the cluster of positive ions is brightly luminous and travels at high speeds. Both positive and negative streamers move between the electrodes so that discrete balls of light move in various directions.

In air at high field strengths, the normal colour of the streamers is a bright blue, since the most frequent radiation is from highly excited nitrogen (N_2) molecules. Ultraviolet (UV) radiation is also produced, and its intensity exceeds that of blue in most cases.

In our studies, some colours other than blue and white were observed with lengthy discharges, when deposits of organic matter and water vapour were allowed to build up on the transparent electrode. Cleaning of the electrode produced immediate change back to solely blue and white.

People have observed red, orange, yellow and, rarely, even green splotches appearing amongst the blue and white colour, especially after what has been reported to be an emotional or psychic experience. An explanation is easily arrived at by considering the structure of colour film: it is composed of three pigment layers, blue, green and red in that order, with the blue on the emulsion side and the red adjacent to the film support. We felt that if film buckling or film vibration occurred, streamers would develop between the electrode and the back of the film as well as at the front. What enters the back will expose red and green layers to some degree, providing colour production in the orange range with variations to the red and yellow side depending upon the preponderance of UV or blue light generated by the streamer.

The fact that people using Polaroid film with a stiff opaque backing never see anything except blue and white is consistent with the film-gap postulate. In addition, our experiments with the transparent electrode reveal only blue and white patterns. Finally, a direct series of experiments with UV light entering the back of the film completely confirms that one is able to generate the entire range of colours just by changing the intensity and exposure time. In addition, by using a finger pad in contact with the emulsion side of a colour film and by varying the distance between the driving electrode and the back side of the film, one is able to generate the entire range of patterns and colours reported by anyone in this field.

Rational Expectations

Is it rational to hope to observe a nonphysical manifestation directly, using only instruments fashioned after the five physical senses? I think not. We can expect only to detect information at the physical level. By nonphysical energies is meant energies of a nonelectromagnetic, nonsonic and nongravitational variety; energies that do not directly stimulate our five physical senses, and energies that do not propagate in the four-dimensional space-time continuum. There are three categories of devices one may use for monitoring nonphysical energies: (a) a human being who has already developed other sensory systems makes observations with them and provides a verbal readout (a medium), (b) a living system (animal, plant or human) plus an attached electromagnetic or mechanical device, so that the living system transduces the nonphysical energies into readout via a purely physical path (Kirlian devices); and (c) a totally inanimate device based upon a different logic system than that which we call the physical, which acts both as a transducer and a readout mechanism (no instruments in this category).

As the Kirlian device falls in the middle category, we should not be at all surprised (or dismayed) to find a perfectly reasonable physical explanation for the generation of light and for the colour observations. The important and difficult step is to prove that such observations are indeed directly correlated with energy changes in the living system, rather than just the random fluctuations associated with inadequate experimental technique. This has not yet been proved one way or the other.

In a recent *Time* magazine article it was pointed out that "doubt" is the most valuable weapon in the arsenal of the truth seeker. One cannot deny the general wisdom of this statement; however, the timing of the application of doubt is extremely critical, especially in psychoenergetic investigations.

If nature is constructed in the way physicist Sir James Jeans suggests—"The universe begins to look more like a great thought than a great machine"—then the state of our minds at the time of the experiment should exert an influence on the experiment. Our best procedure would then be to project a positive and supportive attitude during the running of a well-planned experiment and to reserve our critical attitudes and doubts for later when we are reflecting on the data. In this way we have a better chance of observing these psychoenergetic manifestations.

This is also the reason why most of those studying parapsychology can be listed in the category of "believers." They would need to be in order to have a reasonable chance of manifesting positive results. Of course, they must also have a well-developed critical faculty and the personal honesty to use it at the proper time for evaluating the meaningfulness of their own data.

Mental Bias Part of Procedure?

We should recognise that the "scientific method" does

not require one to be coldly objective and critical during an experiment, but rather requires one to develop a necessary and sufficient experimental protocol for obtaining a consistency relationship via the experiment no matter who does it and where it is performed. Thus, if a positive mental or emotional bias is helpful in obtaining certain results, it may indeed be a very necessary part of the experimental protocol. But it must be specified and measured.

To move forward and reliably identify psychoenergetic effects via high-voltage photography, we must carefully monitor those physiological parameters than can directly influence the streamer process and which can be altered by mental or emotional changes in the living organism. These appear to be at least five-fold: (1) large changes in the electrostatic potential of the skin, (2) changes in skin chemistry, (3) changes in the dielectric properties of the skin, (4) changes in the secondary electron emission characteristics from the skin and (5) changes in the overall electrical impedance of the system.

To do this job properly, it will be necessary to develop high-voltage photography devices that control and vary the applied voltage, pulse duration, pulse repetition rate, radio frequency under the pulse, electrode spacing, gas chemistry, etc. In addition, one will need to independently monitor the discharge current, skin chemistry, capillary blood flow, etc. In this way, it should be possible to develop a reliable and useful life-energy monitoring device of value to both medicine and parapsychology.

20

THE SCHLIERAN SYSTEM—
AN AURA DETECTOR?

Sheila Ostrander and
Lynn Schroeder

In the future we naturally can expect that new photographic techniques will be used in energy field research. Ostrander and Schroeder present an account of a method known as Schlieran photography, which may provide a number of correlations between clairvoyant perception of the aura and scientific findings. However, many physicists do not yet feel confident that either Schlieran color or monochrome photographs can be decisively evaluated quantitatively. This note of caution will no doubt prompt psi researchers to be more careful in their conclusions.

* * *

Surveys of individuals who claim to see auras describe the aura as a pulsating, moving field, composed of one or many colors, around the human body. The colors are said to vary according to the health, emotions, or thoughts of the subject. According to a *Fate Magazine* survey conducted by Louis J. Vacca, respondents see first a narrow dark band, one quarter inch wide next to the skin. Beyond this, projecting from two to four inches, they see a second aura, the inner aura, which they said was very clear. Past this region of the energy envelope they perceived a third aura, misty and without sharp outlines, extending out six to eight inches.

The two-to-four-inch inner aura is only faintly colored—silvery, greenish, or golden, they told the pollster. Some respondents reported that *"the inner aura is similar to heat waves shimmering up from the pavement on a hot day."*

This description given by aura-seeing individuals is strikingly similar to observations being made by contemporary scientists studying heat convection currents surrounding the human body. Normal body heat creates currents that form a pulsing envelope of warm air from one to three inches thick. This layer is warmer than the general environment; and, though invisible to most of us, it shows up as a halo on photographic plates, using a nineteenth-century German technique, called Schlieren photography, developed to detect flaws in glass. When the convection currents are made visible by the Schlieren system, the envelope of warm air around the body appears as a "shimmering, rainbow-colored aura," according to David Heiserman of *Science Digest*.

A team of doctors at the City University of London, led by Dr. Harold E. Lewis, discovered that this "heat" aura is laden with bacteria, particles of inorganic matter, and microscopic bits of skin. This halo contains up to 400 percent more micro-organisms than the immediate environment and may explain formerly unaccountable inhaled doses of airborne bacteria, says Dr. Lewis. Experimenters have also theorized that some diseases hang on because the envelope of warm air tends to trap bacteria and act as a breeding ground for them.

Does this heat envelope around the body correspond to the field psychics perceive? Or could its action pattern be similar?

Schlieren photography, which is also used to study airflow in supersonic wind tunnels, is now revealing some fascinating things about the pulsating warm airflow around the human body. Just as a prism breaks up light into a band of colors, convection currents in air can also break up light into color patterns. Each layer of air in the human air envelope has its own color, depending on its density and temperature. The Schlieren optical system makes these color patterns visible on a screen.

An American psychiatrist with psychic ability, Dr. John Pierrakos, director of the Institute for Bioenergetic Analysis in New York, has studied the energy fields of the body for some fifteen years, simultaneously with his medical practice. He believes these energy fields, which he is able to perceive psychically, are tied up with the body's metabolism, heat, emotions, rate of breathing, and with humidity, atmospheric conditions, and other factors.

Dr. Pierrakos psychically perceives a kind of "corpuscularlike movement" of small particles in this four-inch inner aura. As part of a complex, detailed description of this pulsating, shifting field around a human subject, he observes, ". . . the field moves from the ground up on the inner side of the legs and thighs, up the trunk and outer side of the hands, forearms, and arms. The two mainstreams meet and travel upwards towards the neck and over the head. At the same time there is a movement at the inside of the lower and upper extremities towards the ground."

Researchers at the City University of London used the Schlieren optical system to research and photograph the convection currents around the human body, and here's what they see happening: "Starting at the soles of the feet, the air layer moves slowly upward over the body. At the groin and under the armpits it reverses direction briefly. At the shoulders it spurts upward to dissipate in a feathery plume about five inches above the head. Both psychic and scientist now claim you have a halo! Classic descriptions of the auras of the hands indicate there are bands of energy between the fingers and rays of energy projecting from each finger. Schlieren photographs show a similar pattern, perhaps again revealing some aspect of the aura or providing an analogy to it.

Could these warm-air convection currents play a role in what some people are seeing as the inner aura? Could this flowing heat envelope be functioning in a similar way to the actual aura, following the flow patterns of auric energy fields? Certainly the surround of colored energy around the body made visible by the Schlieren system may be *only a part* of what psychics see, yet there are a number of similarities. Perhaps coordinating what psychics see with what the Schlieren system reveals might provide more clues about aura diagnosis—there may be certain patterns in the heat aura that match anomalies in the psychic aura.

Aside from the basic flow pattern of the auric energy up from feet to head and down again, Dr. Pierrakos also observes that there is an alternate upward and downward movement of the aura in each half of the body: ". . . The field pulsates from the midsection of the body towards the head and feet simultaneously both in the front, back, and the sides of the body," he says.

The overall movement of the aura energy he sees can roughly be represented by a figure eight crossing over the solar plexus. He finds that each individual has an energy of a different tone, rhythm, color, and vibration. These luminous forces around the body "thunder" and "quake" with strong emotions, he says. Especially anger and rage seem to make them cascade like an avalanche. In diagnosing from energy fields, he looks for blockages, deflections of energy, change of flow pattern, dull color, slowing of vibratory movements.

That a medical doctor should be able to perceive these auric energy fields and diagnose from them is not all that unusual, according to Dr. Shafica Karagulla in her intriguing book, *Breakthrough to Creativity*. Many of her colleagues were willing to confide in Dr. Karagulla, a medical doctor herself, and revealed their unusual "secret" ability to perceive beyond the range of the normal.

Many doctors, like the outstanding diagnostician she met from the Mayo Clinic, could instantly perceive the energy fields of patients and check for pathology the movement the person walked in, though to protect their medical standing they said nothing and put the patient through routine lab tests. She encountered a large number of doctors and psychics across America who, like Dr. Pierrakos, see a living, moving web of energy frequencies involved with the body. Some also saw vortices of energy at certain points along the spine connected with the endocrine system. Says Dr. Karagulla, "You begin to get a picture of man only as a dense physical form, but man made up of several types of energies, and that the solid form is the by-product—the final condensation —rather than the primary factor."

It may be that scientific instrumentation such as the Schlieren system might show the *effects* of the auric energy on the heat envelope around the body. Just as psychics claim to be able to diagnose from examining the aura energy patterns, doctors researching with the Schlieren system have found they can also diagnose from the body energy patterns.

They found striking changes of color in the heat sur-round that coincide with an increased bacteria count due to infection and unusual changes in the flow pattern that coincide with areas of inflammation. Observing the flow pattern of the heat aura they discovered that the bac-teria-laden warm air flowed toward the nose where it was inhaled—possibly accounting, they thought, for certain bacterial and viral infections such as the asthma attacks children get after eczema. Illnesses, such as arthritis, for instance, in which joints become inflamed, cause a rise in heat in certain areas and changes in the flow of convec-tion currents. Doctors have already succeeded in map-ping body temperatures with a heat-detecting instru-ment called a thermograph to provide an early diagnosis system for rheumatoid arthritis at its earliest stage, when crippling is most preventable.

Dr. Glen W. McDonald of the U.S. Department of Health, Education and Welfare says that every human body emits infrared radiation. "If the eyes were struc-tured to see this emission," he added, "each of us would have an incandescent glow." The thermograph can "see" this glow. And because areas of inflammation emit more heat than other regions, the glow from such joints is different from normal glow.

Though science has so far begun to make visible just a part of the vast sea of energies psychics perceive around us, nevertheless even this expansion of perceptions has paid dividends—Could combining data from thermograph maps and Schlieren pictures help give us an analogy of what and how psychics diagnose from the aura?

Would a psychic's description of his perception of a subject's inner aura coincide with the shimmering currents made visible by the Schlieren technique? A person suffering with an inflammatory disease such as arthritis might first be looked at by psychics, to study the effects of the inflammation on the energy flow of the inner aura, and then studied with the Schlieren technique.

In addition, could the Schlieren technique help make visible changes occurring during various kinds of psi phenomena? Human relations constitutes another fascinating area that could be investigated to see whether the psychics see the same thing the optical system amplifies. Dr. Pierrakos says, "If you could see this luminous and colorful phenomenon around the body and between people, you certainly would have the feeling that people swim in a sea of fluid with brilliant colors which constantly change and vibrate." It would be interesting, too, to coordinate Schlieren-aura findings with other research on the aura and Kirlian photos.

21

WILHELM REICH AND ORGONE: THE BACKGROUND

W. E. Mann

Systematic investigation of energy fields will increasingly draw scientists into a closer look at theories and data, proposed by those who have postulated energies that appear to have a direct bearing on what has been defined as the aura, and who have been condemned in the past as charlatans or ignored as overambitious eccentrics. It therefore isn't surprising that there is a considerable revival of interest today in the awesome work of Wilhelm Reich.

Ted Mann, professor of sociology at York University in Toronto, presents us with a brief introduction to Reich and "orgone."

* * *

Since the famous formula of Einstein and the production of nuclear energy, the twentieth century has emerged as the century obsessed by energy. The day-to-day operation of a technological civilization demands this preoccupation, as does man's restless, energy-draining search to conquer more of nature. It was both logical and less anxiety-creating that the early inquiries were focused on energy in the universe and in matter, and only much later began to accept living organisms and man as energy systems. After the First World War, philosophy in the person of Bergson elaborated a vitalistic perspective, but not till recently have many scientists concentrated on the energies that lie within and drive organisms. The elucidation and application of such vitalities may lead to a "bomb" as potent in its own way as that exploded at Hiroshima.

One man who became obsessed by the question of vital energies in organisms, nature and man was the German-born psychoanalyst colleague of Sigmund Freud, Dr. Wilhelm Reich. During his lifetime—he died in 1957—his numerous books and articles on what he called orgone energy excited both interest and considerable persecution. Now, some fifteen years later, one finds new interest in him and his orgone theory.

The difficulties of grappling with the orgone-energy theory are partly illuminated by a simple sketch of Reich's professional career. In 1919 he attached himself—at the age of twenty-two, and while still attending medical school—to that way-out, exotic group of agnostic Jews who, clustering around Sigmund Freud in Vienna, laid the groundwork for the profession of psychoanalysis. Among their contemporaries, Freud and his eager disciples were regarded as kooks, oddballs, freaks, out to sexualize the world. How Freud won acceptance for his unorthodox ideas, and how psychoanalysis—which began in Austria and Germany—became a "big thing" in the United States is in itself a fascinating story, a story commented on by biographers and in-group members, but still lacking definitive sociological treatment.

Beginning as an enthusiastic follower of Freud, Wilhelm Reich became a devoted colleague and was stimulated to launch some distinguished and independent work in the late twenties. A vigorous member of the International Psychoanalytic Association and a practicing analyst, he wrote a number of well-received articles and then several books before he turned thirty. Within this fringe group of alienated intellectuals, he became the leader of those committed to (1) integrating Marx and Freud, and (2) combining theory and clinical work with practical preventive efforts to erase human neuroses. As early as 1929, for example, he joined the Communist party and began to operate sex-hygiene clinics in Berlin and elsewhere, designed to free proletarian youth from puritan and authoritarian hangups. (These might be called sex information clinics today.) Arthur Koestler, in *The God That Failed*, commented on his contact with Reich in a Berlin Communist cell; he said: "Only through a full uninhibited release of the sexual urge could the working class achieve its revolutionary potentialities and historic mission; the whole thing was less cockeyed than it sounds."

By 1930 Reich had become too independent for Freud, and they began to grow apart. Reich's emphasis on the importance of negative transference (and its handling) for psychoanalytic therapy, and on character armoring and orgastic potency as the test for therapeutic success was putting a serious strain on Freud's friendship. By 1934 he had proved too deviant for both the German Communist party and the International Psychoanalytic Association, and each in its own way unceremoniously kicked him out. His criticisms of "red Fascism" in Russia and of Freud's death-wish theory were prominent reasons for his rejection by these two movements.

By 1935, Wilhelm Reich, now a refugee from Nazi Germany, wandered around Europe anxiously looking for a professional home and a new and secure perspective. He determined to discover the physical character of the libido energy that Freud early postulated. In Norway he engaged in lab experiments measuring the electrical components of various forms of sexual interaction. . . . Subsequent investigation led to the discovery of what he called "bions"—basic life-energy units—and the origin of a new field of study, biophysics and orgone (life) energy. By 1938, these researches had aroused the ire of the Norwegian press, and he was forced to sail for America, which became for him "The Promised Land." Rejected by the bulk of European psychoanalysts, he became marginal to that highly marginal medical group, psychoanalysis, and ended up in New York a marginal man in the land of liberty, heretics and outcasts.

Initially he lectured at the radical and, at that time, not widely recognized New School for Social Research, in New York. . . . Meanwhile, he developed the concept of orgone energy and began experiments to test orgone's effect on cancer, using various kinds of orgone-energy accumulators. Efforts to get Albert Einstein to validate the existence of this new energy, launched in December, 1940, ended in dismal failure within a few months.

Around 1945 Wilhelm Reich added to his isolation and ultimately to his eccentricity by leaving New York to settle on farm property near the tiny town of Rangeley, Maine. There he built a small laboratory, gathered around himself a few score followers—mostly unconventional doctors, psychiatrists and oddballs—and delved further into the secrets of his orgone energy.

In 1947, partly as a result of two inaccurate articles by Mildred Brady, a free-lance journalist writing in the *New Republic* and *Harper's*, Wilhelm Reich was suddenly labeled dangerous and a schizophrenic. Behind this attack were some uneasy psychiatrists and psychoanalysts. Even the Menninger Clinic leaders accepted the Brady story as reliable. Soon, the United States Government's Food and Drug Administration began an investigation of his orgone accumulator, which he now claimed to be useful in cancer therapy but not a cure. As his permissive views on sex for teen-agers, written in the early thirties, leaked out, circulation-hungry magazines put out sensational, often inaccurate and usually "put-down" articles. . . .

Somewhere around 1950, Reich became labeled among the United States medical fraternity as a quack. The orgone accumulators, rented out for ten dollars a month to, at most, several hundred users, mainly doctors and therapists, were supposedly bringing in a lot of money and doing nothing for the patients. (The income was used for research expenses.) Now, completely outside regular medicine as well as psychiatry and psychoanalysis, Reich, with his own journal, printing house and band of followers called medical orgonomists, had become totally marginal. In 1949 he tried to test the power of the orgone to control atomic energy, but the resultant intermixture produced physically dangerous effects to his band of experimenters, and some of his followers quit in anger or fear.

During the fifties things went from bad to worse. In 1954, the Food and Drug Administration closed in, suing him for mislabeling the accumulator as a cancer cure. He fought the charge fiercely, claiming the Government had no right to persecute him for what were purely scientific activities. Rather than defend himself against the specific charges of the Government, he lashed back at them, antagonized and then lost his own lawyer and finally refused to enter the court for the trial. He was finally convicted on a contempt-of-court charge and was sentenced to two years in a Federal prison. Shortly after, one of his close associates killed himself and some of his close followers began to wonder about his mental health. The English radical schoolmaster, A. S. Neill, of Summerhill, a close friend to the end, admitted he could not follow Reich into certain latter-day applications of the orgone theory. His circle of friends and followers diminished. This meant that during the years when he expanded the orgone theory to include meteorological and cosmic forces and even flying saucers, the circle of potentially friendly critics dwindled. Those left were mainly too conscious of his greatness to be critical of grandiose theory building. Then, when he was put in prison, the Government also burned or tried to confiscate all his books that mentioned the orgone. When, nine months later, he died in prison, it seemed the end of a once brilliant but—to many persons—very unstable eccentric.

For twenty-five years the widely accepted view of Wilhelm Reich was that he had written a masterful and original book in *Character Analysis* and that other early work showed brilliance but that with the orgone-energy theory he had "gone off his rocker." The idea of a cosmic life energy as the essential element in all biological life was dismissed as the fond creation of a good mind over-wrought with the need to physicalize Freud's abstract concept of the libido.

22

ELECTRO-DYNAMIC MAN

Vincent H. Gaddis

The "electro-dynamic theory of life" proposed by world-renowned embryologist Harold Saxton Burr and philosopher F. S. C. Northrop was published in 1935 but is only now beginning to receive the scientific attention it merits. This theory, like Reich's "orgone," to a great extent owes its revival to the growing interest in energy fields and aura research. The "electro-dynamic" properties of man, as this selection reveals, have profound implications for the understanding of our intimate relationship to the universe. Vincent Gaddis is a prolific writer on psychic phenomena and a semi-professional magician.

* * *

Man, along with all living things on this planet, has an electrical field. Although the existence of electricity in living matter has been known since the days of Luigi Galvani, it is only during the last few decades that research in this realm has revealed startling discoveries and far more astounding possibilities. And this electricity is identical to that found in the inorganic universe where it represents properties variously called electromagnetic, electrodynamic or electric force fields.

The "electro-dynamic theory of life" was evolved by Dr. Harold S. Burr (E. K. Hunt Professor of Anatomy, Yale University) and Dr. F. S. C. Northrop (Sterling Professor of Philosophy and Law, Yale). They decided that since particle physics in non-living matter had to be supplemented by field physics, the same must be true in organic matter. Thus living organisms composed of atoms and molecules in which complex chemical interchanges were constantly taking place required a force capable of directing and holding together these particles.

In 1935, Dr. Burr, in association with Drs. C. T. Lane and L. F. Nims, perfected an ultra-sensitive microvoltmeter which could measure currents as feeble as a millionth of a volt between two points on or within a living organism. These instruments revealed that all living things had electrical fields of varying intensity. An extensive research program was launched, involving many types of life and hundreds of human subjects.

It was found that force fields in organisms change in strength and polarity in response to internal (biologic) and external (cosmologic) events. These cycles of biorhythms, called "field profiles," were first observed in trees. Then, after plotting more than 30,000 force field profiles from 430 human subjects at Yale, Duke and the University of Pennsylvania Schools of Medicine, as well as at the Roanoke and Downey V. A. Hospitals, similar rhythmic variations were discovered. These studies opened the door to long and short-range predictions in time.

Dr. Leonard J. Ravitz, a neuro-psychiatrist with the Section of Neuro-Anatomy at Yale, took daily readings of eleven students for more than a year. His report (*Yale Journal of Biology and Medicine*, 1951) disclosed that voltage-change cycles correlated roughly with the lunar phases, with peaks appearing when the moon was full, and when it was new. Other cycles brought daily voltages to a peak in December and to a low stable valley in mid-summer. This could be correlated with the sun, which is closest to the earth in mid-December and farthest away in June. These cycles were confirmed in the later, more extensive tests.

Oysters open and close their shells with the rising and falling of the tides. Dr. Frank A. Brown, Jr., of North-western University, took some oysters from a sound near New Haven, Connecticut, and placed them in a tank of salt water at Evanston, Illinois. The temperature was kept constant, the water on an even level, and the room illuminated with a dim, steady light.

For two weeks the oysters opened and closed their shells in time with the tides in New Haven. This indicated that the rhythm was inherited.

After fourteen days the rhythm ended. Hours passed by. Then a new rhythm began. The oysters opened their shells when the full moon stood at zenith over Evanston, when there would have been high tide in Evanston if the city had been on the sea coast. It was the moon's position that influenced the oysters. But what signal, what intermediary force, caused the four-hour change in rhythms?

Charts in the Yale report reveal that the patterns of voltage-changes in trees parallel those of human subjects. Occasionally one chart appears to be the mirror image of the other.

The studies offer strong evidence that the old belief in a relationship between the new and full moon and abnormal mental conditions, such as insanity, is based on truth. Increasing unrest among psychiatric patients at such periods is indicated by augmented voltmeter readings. If disturbances do occur, they generally reach a climax at the time of the increased electrical potentials.

In addition to the seasonal and lunar rhythms, there are other cycles, diurnal and semi-monthly, and fluctuations seemingly connected with changes in the earth's magnetic field. Most of these changes in the earth's field are the result of forces from outer space—cosmic and gamma rays, sunspot radiation and other electromagnetic waves which bombard our planet and our bodies. Some of these forces influence our weather, and hence our emotional states and behavior.

Dr. Ravitz has found that strong emotions cause increases in voltmeter readings. On the other hand, there is a decline in sleeping, narcosis and hypnosis. Differences under phenobarbital narcosis are less marked than under hypnosis, but they are measurable. For the first time the degree of hypnosis can be measured, and in this state the voltage pattern is much more stable than when the subject is in a normal state.

In 1958, at the first annual meeting of the American Society of Clinical Hypnosis, Dr. Ravitz presented a possible neural basis for hypnosis. He pointed out that during this state there are profound electrical alterations in the old centers of the brain. In contrast, the functions are intact and accelerated in the new centers—the neocortex—the area largely concerned with discrimination, reason, judgment and volitional control.

During natural sleep the centers, both old and new, "go to sleep." In hypnosis the old centers "go to sleep," while the new centers "stay awake." Dr. Ravitz suggests that the primary function of the old centers may be that of a dynamo whose electric output is reduced to be directed as energy to the new centers. The old brain would thus store and supply energy, which has to reach a certain level before neocortical activity is possible. This would explain the accelerated thinking and other phenomena frequently evident in hypnotic states.

In general, periods of high voltage are related to irritability, tension and emotion, periods of low voltage with a sense of well-being and contentment. Thus the emotional and behavior cycles in humans are apparently connected with their force field cycles. Forecasting of emotional cycles is therefore possible and in some cases has been successful. This is especially true in the case of psychotic patients who usually have higher readings and are more easily affected emotionally than normal persons.

We live and move in a pulsating sea of energies in which our organisms serve as receivers, transformers and projectors. The electrodynamic theory of life suggests a universal electric field affecting living matter, while, in turn, all life exerts its own influence upon the field while still responding to it. Each individual is thus related to all life, to the earth's magnetic field, and through it to the changes in the electrical fields of the moon and sun. We are a part of the universal whole, influenced by the ceaseless ebb and flow of the universe.

This does not mean that we are mechanistic puppets. Our responses may have common characteristics, but each individual possesses a unique makeup, and his reactions to all influences will be unique.

The implications and probable future discoveries in this new field of expanding research are staggering. Today electrical diagnostic tools are used in medicine, the cycle of ovulation can be determined, and potential vigor in seeds can be measured and electronic treatment of seeds increases powers of germination.

Tomorrow's research may cure insanity, speed up healing processes and bridge gaps between the sciences. It may explain such mysteries as animal migrations and the homing instinct; the controversial auras and strange micro-emanations from organisms that Russian scientists claim to have photographed. It may explain extrasensory perception and much that is puzzling in psychic phenomena. It is, in fact, an important clue to the ultimate mystery of life, and may upset some current physiological concepts.

Where, for example, are the electrical potentials found in the readings generated? Does the answer lie in cell chemistry or in external energy fields? What or where, in fact, is the source of energy we use constantly in our daily activities?

In 1956, Professor Ralph W. Gerard, of the University of Michigan, and A. A. Geiger, of the Neuro-Psychiatric Institute, Chicago, challenged the theory that the brain and central nervous system obtained their energy from the burning of sugar with oxygen. Their report offered evidence that the brain uses something else for its immediate fuel, although they had not discovered the nature of this source.

Today ATP (adenosine triphosphate) is considered the

key source of energy in biological systems. Dr. Carl
Sagan, a Harvard astronomer and exobiologist, reports
that after irradiating certain organic molecules with ultraviolet light in the presence of phosphorous salts, he
has produced small amounts of ATP.

Recent research in molecular biology is bringing science closer to the fundamental chemistry of life. It is now
known that DNA (deoxyribonucleic acid) and RNA
(ribonucleic acid), found only in the nuclei of living cells,
control heredity. DNA consists of four kinds of molecular subunits (called nucleotides), each having a base of a
single   substance—adenine,   thymine,   guanine   or
cytosine.

Life, as we know it, requires protein molecules for
growth. Each molecule is composed of one or more of
about twenty kinds of amino acids hooked together in
long chains, the precise order of which determines what
the protein creates—flesh or bone, hair or feathers.

The theory is that DNA uses its four bases in hundreds
of thousands of "codes," which determine the order in
which amino acids are chemically joined in making protein. RNA molecules, which also have four bases, apparently transfer the codes from the DNA master pattern
(which remains in the cell nucleus) to points within the
cell where they gather amino acids and direct their formation. The DNA molecule has the ability to make an
exact copy of itself which permits cell division and growth
of the organism.

In amino acid molecules, the four elements of life
—carbon, oxygen, hydrogen and nitrogen—are so well
matched in their electrical charges that they are exceptionally stable, and could well have survived the chemical
chaos of elemental times.

In attempting to determine how inorganic elements
became organic matter on earth long ago, scientists have
apparently succeeded in duplicating some of the probable steps. One of the most fascinating was performed in
1953, at the University of Chicago.

Dr. Harold C. Urey, the atomic scientist and Nobel laureate, reasoned that the atmosphere of a primordial planet would be rich, not in oxygen, but in ammonia, methane, hydrogen and water. He wondered what would happen if these substances were placed in a jar and penetrated repeatedly by electrical charges. The experiment was carried out by his student, Dr. Stanley L. Miller, and they were delighted to find that amino acids had been formed.

Thus the first spark of life on our planet may have been lightning—atmospheric electricity—flashing from dawn-age clouds to a turbulent earth.

With this background, let us review some of the luminescent, magnetic and electric anomalies that exist or have existed among animals and men. It is well known that bioluminescence is a characteristic of numerous types of marine life from squids to plankton, chick beetles, glow worms, certain fungi and bacteria and the familiar firefly.

While the reason fireflies light up on summer nights —to attract fireflies of the opposite sex—has long been known, it is only recently that the chemical process involved has been discovered. In the insect's tail are two chemicals, luciferin and the enzyme luciferase, which will glow when brought into contact with ATP. A nervous impulse triggers the reaction. ATP converts chemical energy into mechanical energy, and it is responsible for muscular contractions. In the case of the firefly, it converts chemical energy into light.

Since ATP is present in all living organisms, a current NASA (National Aeronautics and Space Administration) project is to rocket aloft an instrument containing luciferin and luciferase to determine if there is life floating in the stratosphere. If any microbes are picked up, their ATP should cause the chemicals to light up. This light would then be detected by a photomultiplier tube, and the information radioed back to earth. Should microorganisms be detected, NASA will have to find a method of

~~protecting planet-bound spacecraft from contamination~~ after launch.

In human beings, cases of luminescence are rare but varied. Drs. George M. Gould and Walter L. Pyle, in their monumental works, *Anomalies and Curiosities of Medicine*, list the following examples: luminous perspiration, urine and ulcers; two cases of luminous breath, issuing from the mouths of patients shortly before death; two cases of phthisis in which the heads of the victims were surrounded by phosphorescent lights; and a victim of psoriasis, who was enveloped in a luminous aura for several days.

In another case, a woman suffering from cancer of the breast showed a luminosity of the sore which was so strong it could be seen several feet away, and the hands on a watch could be read at night a few inches away.

In the *Annales des Sciences Psychiques* (July, 1905), Dr. Charles Fére tells of two cases he observed of luminous halos appearing about the heads and hands of two female patients—one a woman of a neuro-arthritic family, subject to hysterical symptoms; the other suffering only from severe headaches. In both instances the appearances had an orange tint and lasted for about two hours.

In 1934, world-wide publicity was given to the case of Signora Anna Monaro, an asthma patient in the hospital at Pirano, Italy. Several times a night while she slept, a flickering bluish glow emanated from her breasts, remaining visible for several seconds. During the appearances, her breathing and heartbeats quickened, and afterwards perspiration drenched her body. Since the phenomenon continued over a period of weeks, it was observed by a number of physicians, scientists and government officials. Later she was brought to the Rome Psychiatric Clinic, but by that time the luminosity had vanished.

Dr. Carlos Saiz, a psychiatrist, said he thought the phenomenon was "caused by electrical and magnetic organisms in the woman's body developed in eminent degree." More precise in his definition of "organisms," another doctor suggested the "electromagnetic radiation (came) from certain compounds such as sterols in the skin."

Father Herbert Thurston, in his *Physical Phenomena of Mysticism* (which contains accounts of a number of Roman Catholic saints who are said to have exhibited luminous characteristics), refers to a report on Signora Monaro by Professor Protti to the University of Padua. The professor said the patient had fasted during Lent, which preceded her hospitalization, and that this might have caused the production of an excess of sulphides. Since the radiant power of her blood, which is of an ultraviolet nature, was three times the normal, he suggested that this radiation excited the sulphides.

But there is still another theory. Some years ago, according to Dr. Nandor Fodor, a Professor Dubois in France observed several cases of luminous wounds in "bilious, nervous, red-haired and more often alcoholic subjects." He discovered in the luminous secretions two constituents—luciferin and luciferase. This was, of course, long before the discovoo, at least in some cases of phosphorescent humans, the process may be identical to that displayed by the firefly.

Abnormal radiation of heat from the body seems to be more closely related to sanctity than the other anomalies that are the subject of this chapter. Father Thurston tells of a number of saints who are said to have radiated such heat that it affected material objects and could be painful to other persons.

Without exception this heat was said to be generated within the chest and, more specifically, in the region of the heart. St. Philip Neri, one of the more famous possessing this ability, suffered from heart palpitations during his life. After his death it is said that an autopsy disclosed an enlargement so great that two of his ribs had been broken and thrust outwards.

All of these saints lived long ago, but it has been reported that Padre Pio, the famed Capuchin priest of San
Giovanni Rotondo, Italy, who bears the stigmata, has
such a high temperature at times that clinical ther-
mometers have been broken by the expansion of the
mercury within them.

Turning from west to east, there are the yogis of India
and, particularly, the lamas of Tibet who can exhibit
abnormal heat. Many travelers have told of lamas who
live practically naked in zero temperatures and, while
sitting, radiate such heat that the snow melts around
them. This ability is called *tumo*, and writers on Oriental
mysticism state that its development depends on visuali-
zation of fire, and certain breathing exercises in an environment of high altitudes.

There is no doubt that certain environments contribute to unusual talents. Desert dwellers, without compasses or landmarks develop astonishing directional instincts. In 1957, scientists of the Northern Defense Research Laboratory at Fort Churchill, Manitoba, Canada,
found that Eskimos could hold metal objects in their bare
hands for several seconds in sub-zero weather, while the
flesh of soldiers at the fort froze instantly when they
touched the metal. The tests were inconclusive, but the
investigators found no evidence that the hands of the
Eskimos were tougher or less sensitive to cold than those
of the soldiers.

Some of these abilities are no longer mere curiosities,
but are receiving scientific attention as man faces the
hostile environment of outer space. The concept is that if
we can't modify either the spacecraft or the environment,
we must modify the man.

Dr. Toby Freedman, of North American Aviation,
Inc., is a leader in space medical research. In an interview
with science writer, Albert Rosenfeld (*Life*, October 2,
1964) he strongly advocated studies of man's abnormal
powers. "In the past," he said, "individuals have demonstrated   extraordinary—some   claim,   even   super-

human—powers to resist pain, cold, fire; to survive under fiercely adverse circumstances—without food, without water, buried alive. For the first time science is beginning to investigate such phenomena experimentally and with an open mind."

Since space travel involves problems of pressures and temperatures outside the usual range, Dr. Freedman said the remarkable adaptations of people living in extreme climates demands investigation. He pointed out that Eskimos and Bedouins live in extreme temperatures; and that people in the Andes and the Himalayas lead active lives at heights where the oxygen is sixty percent of our usual requirements.

Continuing, Dr. Freedman referred to Tibetan lamas who are said to be able to maintain normal skin temperature in sub-zero cold, and yogis who are buried alive, and survive on a fraction of normal oxygen consumption. It may not be superstition, he added, since recent experiments have revealed that seals can remain under water for nearly half an hour without breathing, by undergoing systemic changes. A yogi might well develop the ability to perform such changes, and if a yogi could do it, so could an astronaut. Hibernation would enable the astronaut to endure long, boring space journeys.

If man were more durable, spacecraft designing could be greatly simplified. So Dr. Freedman suggests we should develop what he calls Optiman—"a man whose outward appearance is quite normal, but who has been adapted to the oxygen requirements of a Himalayan sherpa, the heat resistance of a walker-on-coals, who needs less food than a hermit, who has the strength of a Sonny Liston, and runs the mile in three minutes flat while solving problems in tensor analysis in his head."

Apparently Soviet scientists have not overlooked this concept. When *Chicago Tribune* reporter Norma Lee Browning returned from Russia in 1963, she announced that along with their extensive research into extrasensory perception (which they call "biological radio communication"), Soviet scientists had "established an exchange program with India to study the physiological and mental disciplines of the yogis."

Static electricity is generated by friction between two unlike substances. When we scuff our feet across a rug on a clear, dry day, a spark of this "baby lightning" will fly from our fingertip when we touch a metal fixture. Static electricity can also be generated by the separation of two substances, resulting in a surge of electrons and protons within the objects.

When we become aware of it, it is static no longer, but has started to go someplace in a hurry. Dry air is a poor conductor, and it allows charges to build up to a voltage which finally jumps to some nearby object. A person walking across a room on a thick rug may store up 10,000 volts; it requires about 20,000 volts to produce a one-inch spark.

The National Safety Council, Inc., has recorded many cases of "human spark plugs" who store up greater voltages than their fellow workers. An oil company driver in Arizona burned up three trucks within a few days before insurance investigators found out that he was highly charged. A woman in a California factory caused seven fires before she was transferred to a safer job. Another woman, working with rubber cement in a shoe factory, accounted for five fires during one winter. She was laid up for three weeks with injuries after the fifth fire. Within fifteen minutes after she returned to her job, a fire started in her cement pail.

Then there are the "human magnets"—spoons and similar metal objects cling to their fingertips, noses or chins. *Anomalies and Curiosities of Medicine* refers to a three-year-old girl who possessed this power. Back in 1938, an elderly woman, Mrs. Antoine Timmer, appeared before a meeting of the Universal Council for Psychic Research at the Hotel New Yorker in the hope of winning some of the $10,000 being offered by psychic phenomena that could not be duplicated by trickery. Spoons defied gravity by clinging to her fingers. But since Joseph Dunninger, the council chairman and a magician, could do the same thing with a concealed thread, Mrs. Timmer returned home without a penny.

Finally there are the "human dynamos"—and some of them are infants. Douglas Hunt, writing in the English magazine *Prediction* (January, 1953), tells of two cases. In one case, the doctor reported that he received an electrical shock while delivering the baby. He was able to charge a Leyden jar from the child and to produce sparks from him. After twenty-four hours, the phenomena ceased. In the second case, the child emanated a faint white light and caused "vibrations" in small metal objects placed near its hands and feet.

A classic case is that of an infant born in 1869 in St. Urbain, France, who was always charged like a Leyden jar. No one could go near him without getting a shock, and luminous rays escaped now and then from his fingers. When he died at the age of nine months a luminous radiance appeared around his body which remained visible for several minutes.

Drs. Gould and Pyle tell of a six-year-old Zulu boy who was exhibited in Edinburgh, in 1882. Anyone touching him received a shock, the intensity variable with the state of the atmosphere. Contact with his tongue gave a still sharper shock.

Much has been written about Angélique Cottin, a French peasant girl who, in 1846, at the age of fourteen, displayed remarkable electrical phenomena for a period of about ten weeks. The first manifestation occurred when the glove-making frame at which she was working began to jump about. Thereafter, her mere approach toward an object, or the touch of her hand on a piece of heavy furniture, sent it spinning.

Angélique was brought to Paris by her bewildered parents, and a number of prominent physicians and scientists observed her bizarre powers. They found that balls of pith, or of feathers hung on silk threads, would be attracted or repelled by the force emanating from her. Compasses were violently agitated in her presence, and when blindfolded, she could distinguish the poles of magnets by her sense of touch. Tables and chairs leaped away from her, even when tightly held by witnesses. Her bed rocked and shook as she slept.

The power was especially strong in the evening, and radiated from the left side of the front of her body, particularly at the wrist and elbow. Her left arm registered a higher temperature than the right. When the phenomena occurred, her muscles convulsed and her heartbeats increased to 120 a minute. The force at times was so great that a sixty-pound table would move if her apron merely touched it. Each time manifestations took place, the girl was seized with fright, and often sought refuge in flight.

Six investigators appointed by the French Academy of Sciences confirmed the phenomena. The commission included François Arago, the famous physicist who received the Copley Medal of the Royal Society in 1825.

Electrical radiation from bodies is rarely so spectacular. During the early 1930s a Count John Berenyi in Budapest, Hungary, received the attention of newsmen. His body was so charged, especially early in the morning, that he could cause neon tubes to glow by holding the terminals. At such times he was also somewhat luminous. Two similar cases were reported in the London *Daily Mirror* (September 16, 1952), the subjects being Charles Bockett, of Port Talbot, and Brian Williams, of Cardiff. They allegedly could make electric lamps glow when held in their hands.

Among human magnets, Louis Hamburger is probably the champion. In 1890, Louis, aged sixteen, was a student at the Maryland College of Pharmacy. He was a well-built youth with unusually fleshy fingers. With the tips of his fingers, which had to be dry, he could pick up heavy objects which were also dry and had a smooth surface. When he placed a number of dressmaker's pins on his open palm and turned his hand over, the pins dangled from his hand, and it required a vigorous shake to loosen them.

His most remarkable feat was to place the tips of three fingers against the side of a glass beaker, containing iron filings, and raise it along with an attached five-pound weight. His fingertips stuck to the beaker with such force that there were audible suctionlike sounds when he pulled them loose.

To Frank McKinstry, of Joplin, Missouri, whose case was reported in 1889, his electricity was a plague. He was over six feet tall, and muscular, but when the charge was at its height after a night's rest, a short walk would leave him helpless. At such times he had to keep moving, for if he stood motionless on the ground for more than a few seconds he became rooted to the spot. When this occurred, someone would pull one of his legs up, then he could move the other foot, and by moving his feet up and down for a minute or so, he would be released. A flash of faint light between his feet and the earth ended the current's grip.

McKinstry was known to be an unusually successful dowser. There may well have been a relationship between this ability and his affliction.

Caroline Clare, of London, Ontario, Canada, was stricken in 1877, when she was seventeen, and doctors were unable to diagnose her trouble. After several months her weight fell from 130 to 90 pounds, and she began suffering from occasional spasms and trancelike states. A year and a half passed by, then she rallied, and her disposition changed from one of melancholy to cheerfulness. With this change came electrical phenomena.

Metal objects clung to her skin. When she reached for a knife, the blade leaped into her hand. After she held any steel object for more than a few seconds, another person had to forcibly pull it from her. Anyone touching her received a shock, and she could shock twenty persons at a time who were holding hands. Objects often in contact with her body, like the metal ribs of her corset, became charged.

As in similar cases, the charge gradually left Caroline, and, over a period of several months, she regained her health. When she reached maturity she was physically normal. A report on her case by attending physicians was presented to the Ontario Medical Association in 1879.

There are other cases of electrified humans, but these examples illustrate that the phenomena do not follow common patterns, and are extremely varied. Before seeking at least a tentative explanation of these cases, there is one more type of phenomenon that should be mentioned: the fire-makers.

In reading works on yoga philosophy, Oriental mysticism and theosophy, one comes across accounts, usually secondhand, of yogis or lamas superphysically producing fire. Such fires are said to be kindled by means of *pratyahara* (meditation) or *mantrayoga* (rhythmic chants). Mme. Alexandra David-Neel, in her *Magic and Mystery in Tibet* (London, 1931), and other writers claim to have witnessed these performances.

In medical records, however, I can find only one case which might be considered analogous. It was reported by Dr. L. C. Woodman in the *Michigan Medical News* in 1882, and there is an account in the *Scientific American*, April, 1883.

The subject was A. W. Underwood, a Negro of Paw Paw, Michigan, whose age was given variously as twenty-four and twenty-seven. He had the ability to take anyone's handkerchief, hold it to his mouth, rub it vigorously with his hands while breathing on it, and it would suddenly burst into flames and be consumed. According to Dr. Woodman, Underwood would strip to the waist, rinse out his mouth thoroughly, submit to a rigorous examination, then proceed immediately to set any cloth or piece of paper on fire with his breath. While out hunting, he would "lie down after collecting dry leaves and by breathing on them start a fire." The doctor added that Underwood could only exert his power twice a day without becoming greatly exhausted.

23.

MY FAITH

Gustaf Strömberg

Former Mount Wilson astronomer Gustaf Strömberg, no doubt strongly influenced by the "electrodynamic theory" proposed by Harold Saxton Burr and F. S. C. Northrop, speculates here on the question of an underlying nonphysical universal order and the "field of organization." Strömberg has "faith" in his belief that "the essence of all living elements is probably immortal," and that "there exists a World Soul or God."

* * *

I believe that behind the physical world we see with our eyes and study in our microscopes and telescopes, and measure with instruments of various kinds, is another, more fundamental realm which can not be described in physical terms. In this nonphysical realm lies the ultimate origin of all things, of energy, matter, organization and life, and even of consciousness itself.

The scientists of the last century believed that our mental activities were the results of the ever-changing configurations and motions of the atoms in our brains. Although this idea is now almost universally abandoned, no alternative theory has been advanced which could explain the relationship and interaction between mind and matter. I am convinced that our consciousness is rooted in a world not built of atoms, and that our mind in its many facets reflects some of the fundamental characteristics of its own origin. Thinking and planning are important characteristics of our mind, and they must then have an origin in a realm beyond ourselves. But we cannot conceive of thinking and planning without a personality that does the thinking and planning. In this way we arrive at the idea of an intelligent and ever-active source or World Soul, very similar to the God of our religion.

Before describing the origin of things and phenomena we must clearly state the difference between physical and nonphysical phenomena. The vibrations of the strings in a musical instrument can be described in physical terms, but our sensations of sound and music belong to another, nonphysical world. The radiation travelling from a source of light to our eyes has physical properties, but our sensations of light and colors are nonphysical. Muscular contractions are physical phenomena, but the will that regulates some of them is incomprehensible from the standpoint of physics.

Where do energy and matter come from? In modern physics matter is regarded as a form of energy, and their ultimate source must therefore be the same. Classical physics has nothing to say about the ultimate origin of energy, but modern physics has given us a hint. The radiation which we picture as travelling from the sun to the earth can be described mathematically as a wave motion, although it should not be regarded as a vibration in a material medium. The "waves" represent in quantitative terms the *chance* of energy emerging at a particular place on the earth. The emergent elements consist of extremely small parcels of energy, which the physicists call *photons*, but the photons themselves can not be considered as moving. The elementary particles of matter have similar properties. *They travel as waves, but act as particles*. Energy can therefore be regarded as emerging from a nonphysical world into the physical world.

In the nonphysical world lies the fountainhead of life. Some of the processes occurring in the living world are apparently governed by conditions that do not exist now but can be expected to prevail in the future. The development of a living organism is in many ways like the building of a machine designed to perform a definite function in the future. A plan must first be made, and this can only be made by an intelligent being with his attention focused, not only on his past experience, but also on the purpose for which the machine is constructed. Nature apparently has foresight and intelligence, and it is capable of highly organized activity. Since an impersonal nature cannot have such characteristics, we are led to the idea of a personal God.

How is organization introduced into the living world? Some twenty years ago it was discovered that in certain animals the general organization started from a particular point in the embryo, a point which the biologists refer to as the dorsal lip of the blastopore. From this point a "wave of organization" appears to spread through the embryo, and its progressing influence can be directly observed as a growth of nerve tissue. Particularly striking are the processes observed during metamorphosis. The "field of organization," which during the life of a larva determined the structure of its body and the functions of its organs, contracts during the pupa stage and disappears, leaving behind a disorganized mass of living cells.

Then a "miracle" happens. A field of organization of a new type expands from a particular point in the mass of living cells and reorganizes the cell system, and the final result is the formation of the complex body of a butterfly. Such organizing, living fields seem to emerge from "another world" into the physical world we study in our microscopes and investigate in our laboratories. There are strong reasons to believe that at death they disappear into the world from which they originally came.

In recent years extensive studies have been made of these organizing fields. The Section of Neuro-Anatomy of the Yale Medical School has been particularly active in this research. All living organisms are imbedded in complex electric fields, and these fields disappear at death. Dr. H. S. Burr, the leader of the research group at Yale, states that it is hard to escape the conclusion that these fields are independent of the matter involved and by their innate properties determine the structure and functions of the living organism.

All our mental characteristics and faculties have their origin in the nonphysical world. There lies the origin of our sensations of light and colors, and of sound and music. There is the origin of our feelings and emotions, and of our will and our thoughts. There is the source of our feelings of satisfaction and bliss, and of guilt and remorse. Our nerve cells seem to be the links which connect our physical brain with the world in which our consciousness is rooted. At death our "brain field," which during our life determined the structure and functions of our brain and nervous system, is not destroyed. Like other living fields it contracts and disappears at death, apparently falling back to the level of its origin. All our memories are indelibly "engraved" in this field, and after our death, when our mind is no longer blocked by inert matter, we can probably recall them all, even those of which we were never consciously aware during our organic life. Some of these memories will torment us, and others will bless us. Our conscience gives us an inkling of what we can expect in another world, where there are pleasure and beauty, as well as sorrow and pain.

This, it seems to me, is the Heaven and Hell indicated by the many new discoveries in modern science.

Epilogue

24.

GHOST UNIVERSE

James Sutherland

While physicists appear to be vigorously demolishing a universe once regarded as "machinelike," researchers are paradoxically demanding better scientific methods to explain psi phenomena. This development should at the very least attract suspicion to any great confidence about well-researched "objective" truth about any psi phenomena. Dealing with "matter" at the atomic level disturbs this confidence as this selection will reveal.

We can expect that any further study of the aura will demand incorporating a more sophisticated philosophical understanding of the implications of quantum physics and relativity, and thereby an acute self-awareness of how one becomes part of the process studied. This attitude will inevitably emerge in the next phase of the growing demand to face up to the extraordinary challenges of "sensitives" and "unorthodox" scientists who continue to view the mystery of the aura as holding the basic key to the meaning of life.

James Sutherland is a graduate student at the State University of New York College of Environmental Science and Forestry at Syracuse, New York. He is interested in the large-scale implications of ecological change upon the world's major population groups.

* * *

A cold night wind bowing the trees, an inexplicable noise in the attic, the hidden backside of the moon: people have always been equally fascinated and scared by things they can't see. Human history is rife with these phantoms. A very old Scottish prayer seeks deliverance from all the shadowy "ghoulies and ghosties and long-leggety beasties, and things that go bump in the night. . . ."

In an early novel, H. G. Wells cannily updated this mixture of curiosity and fear, placed it in the milieu of industrial England and produced an even more powerful concept—an invisible man. The idea of an interloper in our midst, seeing everything while going completely unnoticed himself, is an exceptionally evocative piece of fantasy, but still no more than that. Despite the elaborate rationale Wells worked out for inducing invisibility (drug-treatments) in his character, the whole notion of a transparent human being is one with the ghoulies and the long-leggety beasties in terms of plausibility; some eighty years of scientific research has rendered the concept of invisibility quite untenable. Ironically, the other things that went bump in the dark have been reclassified as "parapsychological phenomena," and gained considerable respect, and now are being investigated by hundreds of university graduate students in this country.

Nevertheless, the ancient curiosity about *things* that people cannot see continues unabated, having split into a pair of divergent lines of inquiry.

The first, and probably the most spectacular, led to the new science of radio astronomy, and, in recent years, the discovery of neutron stars. These aggregations of collapsed matter are so minute in the scale of the universe, they can be detected only with powerful radio receivers tuned to the emission frequency of these objects. Following the disclosure of neutron stars, radio astronomers speculated that even denser invisible stars might exist: the so-called *black holes*, that had gravities so high that they pulled space entirely around them and dropped out of the Universe completely.

The second line of research tended to move in exactly the opposite direction, down a subtle pathway to the tiny and sometimes-paradoxical world that is locked in the center of the atom.

Initially, the atomic nucleus seems like an unpromising starting-point for earnest ghost-hunting. Four generations of high school science instructors have given most people the impression that atoms are actually fairly mundane items: like miniature solar systems composed of electrons, protons and neutrons. It's a neat, tidy concept; and it is something of a shame that that orderly image bears absolutely no relation to reality.

The solar-system-model of the atom is a relic, a hangover from pre-World War II physics that seemingly refuses to die a natural death. It was conceived by an English physicist, Ernest Rutherford, in 1908 to account for a discovery he had made: that the atom is not the smallest particle of matter, but rather is made up of an outer shell and a central core. Rutherford found that the volume of an atom was something on the order of one hundred thousand times the volume of the nucleus. Obviously, there was a lot of empty space inside the atom, and the analogy with the solar system must have occurred to him immediately.

The Danish physicist Neils Henrik Bohr and Rutherford's concept was admirably simple and dramatic: a nucleus "sun" comprised of positively charged protons and chargeless neutrons, around which negatively charged electrons orbited like planets. The proton, neutron and electron were supposed to be the ultimate bits of matter, the three elementary particles.

By the early 1930s the elegant, symmetrical world of the Bohr-Rutherford model had developed several serious drawbacks. It could not explain the erratic behavior of the electrons, which seemed to leap from one orbit to another, then back once more, without actually crossing the space between the orbits. It did not indicate how those electrons could have, simultaneously, the properties of a speck of matter *and* a wave of energy, apparently whenever the electron wanted to. And it was inadequate to describe the odd behavior of the neutron when that particle disintegrated.

Why did it take so long for the weaknesses in the model

of Bohr and Rutherford to show up? There were several reasons, but primarily, it was due to the liberation of thought and imagination by Einstein's theory of relativity which was just then becoming widely accepted. Also, the 1930s marked the introduction of far more precise and sophisticated devices to measure the results of atomic experiments. Miniscule data that had slipped by earlier primitive equipment was detected by the sensitive new recording and counting gear, the likes of which Bohr and Rutherford had never seen in their days.

However, it was still something of a shock when, in 1931, the Austrian physicist Wolfgang Pauli proposed the existence of a *fourth* elementary particle.

It came about in this manner. Pauli, like many physicists of the period, was profoundly disturbed by the peculiar actions involved in the breakdown of neutrons in the atomic nucleus—circumstances observed by dozens of researchers over a span of several years. What bothered them was not so much the fact that the neutron did break down (by this time, they had resigned themselves to the knowledge that their "elementary" particles weren't so ultimate and inviolate after all), but that the Law of Conservation of Energy was being violated.

According to the law, energy can't be destroyed, only relocated.

Yet, a neutron breaking down produced a proton and an electron: when added, their respective energy quotas came out to something less than that of the original neutron. And there was more trouble, too, for the Law of Conservation of Mass dictated that the sum of the masses of the products of such a breakdown should equal the mass of the neutron. Combining the masses of the proton and electron yielded a loss of mass equivalent to a bit less than half that of an electron—for all intents and purposes, that trace of energy and mass had simply vanished into nothingness.

Now this was an unacceptable premise. The two laws were considered to be the major working principles of the Universe, and if they did not hold in this case, they were not true laws at all, but another convenience like the "ether," which Michelson and Morley disproved in 1887.

Pauli resolved this dilemma with an adventurous suggestion. Suppose, he theorized, there is another particle, smaller than an electron that carries the requisite amount of energy with it, but undetectable by our instruments? Such an entity would account for the discrepancies in mass and energy taking place during neutron breakdown, and hence redeem the two laws.

Most physicists accepted Pauli's theoretical particle for that reason, though they probably felt uneasy about admitting a certified ghost into the pantheon of particle physics just to maintain the laws. Soon, though, the particle—named the *neutrino* by Enrico Fermi—came in handy to explain certain other atomic reactions that had previously baffled scientists. Neutrinos were the key to understanding why certain stars suddenly run wild and turn into supernovae, shining briefly with the brilliance of an entire galaxy; previous to the neutrino there was no way to fully account for the incredibly rapid energy changes that occur within these special stars.

Over the years, physicists built up a plausible picture of the neutrino as more and more data about it accumulated. It is, as Pauli predicted, a particle very much smaller than an electron (which was previously believed to be the most minute division of matter possible), but unlike the electron, the neutrino at rest has no physical characteristics other than a somewhat mysterious quality called "spin," which in simple terms means that it behaves as if it were turning on its axis like a tiny gyroscope. Otherwise, the neutrino is a pure ghost, lacking an electrical charge, a magnetic field, or any mass at all!

An entity without mass sounds like a contradiction. Without mass, how can the neutrino be said to exist?

The catch is in the phrase *at rest*. If a neutrino came to a complete stop its mass would be zero. However the neutrino, obviously, never rests; instead, from the moment of its birth during the breakdown of a neutron, the young neutrino is moving at the speed of light. And according to the theory of relativity, as anything approaches the speed of light it acquires mass in proportion to its velocity.

Even though it has some degree of mass, a neutrino is still a ghost in the Universe because it is traveling at the highest possible speed known. Chargeless, non-magnetic, and traveling at 186,000 miles per second, the neutrino treats matter as though it doesn't exist. It will plunge, unaffected, through the Earth in less than a ten-thousandth of a second, or zip blithely into and out of the roiling heart of the sun in only a fraction longer. It makes no difference. To the neutrino, you and I and the remainder of the Universe do not exist.

This is due largely to the fact that atoms contain so much altogether empty space through which the neutrino can pass in its accustomed style. But there is always the chance that a flying neutrino will run smack into another electron, proton, or neutron—or even another neutrino. The odds in favor of such a collision are slight, about one in ten billion, even using a fairly dense object like our Earth as a target.

The odds quoted are depressing indeed until one considers that the number of neutrinos shooting past any particular point also number in the billions. Sooner or later, according to the inexorable rules of statistics, there is bound to be a hit.

Following this sequence of logic produced the very first documented proof that neutrinos exist, that they are more than a felicitous way to preserve some laws of nature.

In 1956, a pair of American physicists, Clyde Cowan, Jr. and Fredrick Reins, announced they had discovered the neutrino in extensive laboratory tests extending over three years by employing the statistical method outlined above. Reins and Cowan found a particularly rich source (in theory) of neutrinos in a nuclear reactor in South Carolina. Atomic fission supposedly would liberate vast quantities of neutrinos by its very mode of operation, which is breaking down atomic nuclei to release energy. The two physicists devised a "neutrino trap" near the reactor: long tanks of water surrounded by hundreds of phototubes.

In several tanks, the water was laced with a special chemical compound that emitted a tiny burst of visible light whenever one of its molecules was struck by an elementary particle. Meanwhile, the phototubes counted each separate scintillation in the tanks. Cowan and Reins were careful to subtract a certain number from the total the phototubes recorded every day; this number represented a statistical estimate of the amount of neutrinos coming in from outside sources other than the reactor. The final figure represented, they hoped, the real number of neutrinos expelled from the reactor.

After more than thirty months, the two physicists matched their totals against the number statistics said *should* have occurred during that period. Both sets matched closely. There was no room for doubt: the neutrino existed. Cowan and Reins had caught their ghost particle.

Later, other physicists and astronomers used a variant of the Reins-Cowan experiment to produce "neutrino telescopes," to measure the number of neutrinos streaming out of the sun, thus providing a valuable clue to the processes taking place in the solar core. In order to shield these odd "telescopes" (actually vats of chlorine compounds in fluid form) from stray radiation of other sorts, these devices are placed at the bottom of mile-deep mines in the U.S. and South Africa. At these depths, only the neutrino can penetrate down to the 'scopes, and there be detected, counted and analyzed.

In the quarter-century between the proposal and the real discovery of the neutrino, the trail of research occasionally led into some far-flung and definitely peculiar areas. One of the strangest of these territories was found to be filled with a different kind of ghost—particles that are mirror-images of the common constituents of our Universe.

The very first elementary particle to be revealed in laboratory experiments was the electron, identified by the English physicist Joseph John Thomson. Thomson, who casually unloaded this bombshell during an evening lecture at the famous Royal Institution on April 30, 1897, determined that the electron was a minute bit of matter, entirely separate from an atom, and bearing a negative charge. Thirty years later, another Englishman, physicist Paul Dirac, suggested that the electron might have a twin brother—possessing identical physical characteristics, save one. According to Dirac's calculation, this particle would be charged positively. It would be an anti-electron.

Dirac had not so long to wait as did Pauli for his theory to be vindicated. An American studying cosmic ray behavior found evidence of Dirac's particle and named it *positron*, a shortened version of positive-electron. The physicist, Carl Anderson, made his announcement in 1932, barely two years from the publication of Dirac's original theory.

The positron was the first evidence of the existence of anti-matter.

As the years passed, physicists found that virtually every subatomic particle had its anti-matter counterpart having either a reversed electric charge or some other mirror-image characteristic. There are anti-protons, anti-neutrons and some fifty others, including an anti-neutrino. The latter particle was also discovered by the Reins-Cowan team in 1956, and has proved useful in making lucid otherwise inexplicable nuclear reactions in the heart of collapsing wildcat stars.

Previously, it was held that because anti-particles were by nature inimicable with ordinary particles, the product resulting from a collision between a positron and electron would be a scattering of gamma rays. In supernovas, however, such a run-in may produce an unexpected duet—a neutrino and an anti-neutrino, which promptly exit the star for regions unknown. This particular reaction is statistically a rare event, but in the superdense center of a star going nova, enough of these odd reactions take place in a space of one or two days that the neutrinos and anti-neutrinos will take with them all the free energy.

Mortally bled, the star crumples, the interior temperature rises to six billion degrees, and the star explodes with inconceivable fury.

But even the power of a supernova is slight compared to the violence that is theorized to occur when a sizable lump of anti-matter contacts normal matter. Astronomers now believe that a few ounces of anti-matter intersected the orbit of the Earth on June 30, 1908, producing what is now known as the Great Siberian Meteorite Impact. (A very recent alternate theory is that a wandering black hole is responsible, slicing directly through the center of the Earth from Siberia, and emerging from the floor of the South Atlantic. It must have raised a spectacular waterspout!)

It is perhaps fortunate that anti-matter remains on the level of subatomic particles, for the most part, in our end of the Universe. There are speculations that another section of the cosmos is constituted entirely of antimatter, even as ours is of what we think of as regular matter. It's only speculation, of course, for there is no way of proving such an anti-Universe does exist, but there is no fundamental reason it could not. With the advent of ultrapowerful linear particle acceleration machines, physicists have been able to create and demonstrate the properties of anti-particles. And experimenters at the Brookhaven National Laboratory in New York State were able to "construct" an antimatter nucleus of the element deuterium in 1965, by combining an anti-proton and an anti-neutron for a slight fraction of a second.

The anti-particles all have extremely short lives, winking in and out of existence in milliseconds or less. Some physicists think this is an anomaly: ordinary particles have long lives, so why should their mirror-images vanish so quickly? It is as though they are not actually "attached" to this Universe, but are instead simply ducking in and out for the benefit of curious physicists.

One curious physicist, Richard Feynman, suggested that what we call a positron is actually an electron that for some reason has become temporally inverted, It is nothing more—or less—than a rather prosaic piece of matter that is travelling into the past instead of moving into the future.

Feynman believed that this tendency to journey backwards in time was necessarily of short duration, because the general flow of time in our end of the Universe is toward the future. It *is* possible to buck the stream, according to the theory, but for only an instant.

Needless to say, Feynman's concept was greeted with mixed enthusiasm. It did answer some perplexing questions about the physical characteristics, but it at once undermined one of the long-standing tenets of physics: the progress of time is in one direction only. By admitting Feynman's theory, physicists and philosophers would have to scrap the cherished principle symbolized by the phrase *time's arrow* and for many that is simply too much, despite the fact that Feynman was awarded the Nobel Prize for his work in 1965. Opponents of the theory have mustered some strong logical objections, which have not yet been either resolved or refuted by Feynman's proponents; the time-travelling hypothesis remains one of the most controversial subjects in science today, and most observers think it may take decades or even centuries of experimentation to decide the issue permanently. It is entirely possible that a final settlement may have to wait until scientists themselves can either create or capture sizable chunks of anti-matter suitable for laboratory analysis—amounts considerably in excess of today's occasional stray ghost particle or two.

Still, even as theory, this is an astonishing advance beyond the atomic model proposed by Neils Bohr and Ernest Rutherford in the early years of this century; that concept now seems positively quaint and naive, considering the viewpoint afforded by neutrinos, anti-matter and time-travelling electrons. If a danger exists in this broader vista of the atom and the Universe, it lies in thinking that the cosmos as depicted by Pauli, Dirac and Feynman is the only one possible. Drawing lines limiting the boundaries of reality is always hazardous and always a failure. Sooner or later another ghost turns up to spoil everything.

Even an *imaginary* ghost can cause quite a stir.

Such was the case with tachyons.

The speed of light in a vacuum is close to 186,000 miles per second, and is generally considered to be the upper limit of velocity in the Universe. Even the neutrino, massless and chargeless and the closest thing to a totally free spirit thought possible, obeys this one Einsteinian rule. Since the Theory of Relativity was announced over fifty years ago the speed of light has been respected as one of the very few inflexible constants in nature.

During the 1960s, however, a few physicists and mathematicians specializing in relativity began to realize that there might be an exception to the cosmic speed limit. One of the most imaginative of this group was a young Columbia University physics professor named Dr. Gerald Feinberg. It was Feinberg's contention that the Theory of Relativity's limitation applies to "ordinary matter and all the other elementary particles." However, the theory does permit the (theoretical) existence of particles that do travel faster than light.

These particles, Feinberg theorized, could exist only on the other side of the light-speed barrier, and their velocities could range from 186,000 mps to infinity. Their single limitation would be this: they could not travel any slower than the speed of light, just as ordinary particles cannot go any faster.

Feinberg named his particles tachyons (from the Greek word meaning swift; surely this is one of the great understatements of our time!), and proceeded to work out some of their supposed characteristics. A "slow" tachyon, flying about at just above c (the speed of light), would contain more energy and momentum than one travelling faster. As the speed of a tachyon approaches infinity its intrinsic energy decreases to nothing, and its total momentum shrinks to a minute percentage close to but never actually zero.

Extrapolating on the last-named property, Feinberg

determined that tachyons would make excellent propul-
sive agents for interstellar spacecraft, employing the particles as a rocket exhaust. A hypothetical engine that
could somehow "make" tachyons out of ordinary matter
would have the capability of reaching 99.9999 etc. per
cent of the value of c. Naturally, the ship could not exceed
c itself because it would be constructed of normal matter
(along with the crew). But next to finding a bona-fide
space warp, the tachyon rocket appears to be the best
hope for commuting around the Milky Way anyone has
yet seriously proposed.

For the present, tachyons are only an attractive
hypothesis: we have no method to determine their existence, and the single definite conclusion to be drawn is
that there is absolutely no theoretical reason tachyons
couldn't exist. Such negative evidence is little consolation
for the person with an itch to get out and explore the
galaxy. It is worth recalling, though, that many other
sub-atomic particles were eventually found simply because nobody could theoretically disprove their being. It
could happen once again.

But in another sense it hardly matters whether there
are such things as tachyons, or positrons. They are ample
reminders that our knowledge is not complete, and never
shall be. The final explication of the Universe is very far
away indeed. And there are probably plenty of ghosties,
ghoulies and long-leggety beasties hanging about, as yet
unnoticed, waiting for their turn.

SELECTIVE BIBLIOGRAPHY

In addition to the main sources used for this anthology, the following are considered important for anyone who wants to further explore the functions and implications of the aura. Also, I have dealt more extensively with many of the issues explored in this book in *Exploring the Human Aura* written in collaboration with Jan Merta (to be published by Prentice-Hall).

Adamenko, V. G. "Electrodynamics of Living Systems." *Journal of Paraphysics*, 4:1970.

Barnothy, Madeleine F., ed. *Biological Effects of Magnetic Fields*. New York: Plenum Press, 1964.

Bolen, James Grayson. "Interview: Shafica Karagulla, M.D." *Psychic*, January/February, 1974.

Burr, Harold Saxton. *Blueprint for Immortality: The Electric Patterns of Life*. London: Neville Spearman, 1972.

Burr, Harold Saxton, and Northrop, F. S. C. "The Electrodynamic Theory of Life." *Quarterly Review of Biology*, 10:322, 1935.

Crookall, Robert. *The Mechanisms of Astral Projection: Denouement After 70 Years*. Moradabad, India: Darshana International, 1969.

Dakin, H. S. *High-Voltage Photography*. 3456 Jackson Street, San Francisco, California 94118, 1974.

Davis, Albert Roy, and Bhattacharya, A. K. *Magnet and Magnetic Fields or Healing by Magnets*. Calcutta: Firma K. L. Mukhopadhyay, 1970.

Fox, Oliver. *Astral Projection*. New York: University Books, 1962.

Garrett, Eileen J. *Awareness*. New York: Berkley, 1968.

Jeans, James. *The Mysterious Universe*. New York: Dover, 1968.

"Kirlian" Electrophotography Data Package. Mankind Research Unlimited, Inc., 1325-1/2 Wisconsin Avenue N.W., Washington, D.C. 20007.

Koestler, Arthur. *The Roots of Coincidence*. London: Hutchinson, 1972.

Krippner, Stanley, and Rubin, Daniel, eds. *Galaxies of Life*. New York: Gordon and Breach, 1973.

Leadbeater, C. W. *The Astral Plane*. Wheaton, Illinois: The Theosophical Publishing House, 1968.

———, *The Chakras*. Wheaton Illinois: The Theosophical Publishing House, 1972.

Muftic, Mahmoud K. *Researches on the Aura Phenomena*. Hastings, England: The Society of Metaphysicians Ltd., 1970.

Osteopathic Physician, The. October 1972 (entire issue).

Owen, A. R. G. "Generation of an Aura: A New Parapsychological Phenomenon." *New Horizons*, 1:1, 1972.

Panchadasi, Swami. *The Human Aura: Astral Colours and Thought Forms*. Hackensack, New Jersey: Wehman Bros., 1940.

Prat, S., and Schlemmer, J. "Electrography." *Journal of the Biological Photographic Association*, 7: 1939.

Presman, A. S. *Electromagnetic Fields of Life*. New York: Plenum Press, 1970.

Ravitz, Leonard J. "Electromagnetic Field Monitoring of Changing State-Function, Including Hypnotic States." *Journal of the American Society of Psychosomatic Dentistry and Medicine*, 17: 1970.

Robinson, Lytle. *Edgar Cayce's Story of the Origin and Destiny of Man*. New York: Coward, McCann and Geoghegan, 1972.

Russell, Edward W. *Design for Destiny*. London: Neville Spearman, 1971. Also available in a Ballantine paper edition.

Scientific Methodological Seminar in Alma-Ata, 1969, Material: *Bioenergetic Questions*. Southern California Society for Psychical Research, Beverly Hills, California.

Sextus, Carl. *Hypnotism: A Correct Guide to the Science and How Subjects are Influenced.* North Hollywood, California: Wilshire Book Company, 1971.

Symposium of Psychotronics, Part III: Seminar on Bioplasm, *Journal of Paraphysics*, 5:4, 1971.

Tiller, William A. "A Technical Report on Some Psychoenergetic Devices." *A.R.E. Journal,* 7: 1972.

READ THE WISDOM AND POWER
OF EDGAR CAYCE